The Prodigal Project

# PRAISE FOR
# THE PRODIGAL PROJECT

If you're tired of the propaganda, *The Prodigal Project* is a must-read. It's the model of what men and women must be and do to find hope, joy, and a future. It's the path forward to save America. Kendall Qualls' story and message are riveting and compelling. This book will give you clarity and hope. It will give you a road map regardless of your skin color. The pages within will change your perspective and your family's future if you apply the wisdom Kendall shares.

—**Dr. Mark Henry,** Lead Pastor of Revive Church,
Brooklyn Park, Minnesota

In the pages of *The Prodigal Project*, Kendall Qualls invites us into his remarkable life and masterfully shares the lessons he learned along the way. Those same lessons can save not only the Black family in America, but all families. This compelling story is surprisingly intimate and impossible to put down.

—**Kimberly Ells,** author of *The Invincible Family:*
*Why the Global Campaign to Crush Motherhood*
*and Fatherhood Can't Win*

In the pages that follow, Kendall bravely pulls back the curtain on the real culprit in Black America. His personal story of poverty, hard work, and resolve serves as a roadmap to success for all. See how the power of faith and persistence are needed to change mindsets and communities across Minnesota and our country.

—**Liz Collin,** Emmy-Award Winning Journalist
and Best-Selling Author

Almost immediately upon meeting Kendall Qualls, I recognized he was a man of rare conviction, leadership, and devotion. He is a family man with a head for business. He is a businessman with a heart for people. He is a leader with the mind of a stoic. All of this comes through in *The Prodigal Project.*

Mr. Qualls' vision is not complicated, nor is it based on trendy academics. It is rooted in integrity, faith, and a genuine desire to see people succeed. It is a refreshing take on the role of family in American society.

—**Michele Tafoya,** Record setting, four-time
Sports Emmy Award winner is the Host of
*Sideline Sanity* on the Salem Podcast Network

HOPE FOR
AMERICAN FAMILIES

# THE
# PRODIGAL
# PROJECT

## KENDALL QUALLS

NEW YORK
LONDON • NASHVILLE • MELBOURNE • VANCOUVER

# The Prodigal Project

## Hope for American Families

Published in New York, New York, by Morgan James Publishing. Morgan James is a trademark of Morgan James, LLC. www.MorganJamesPublishing.com

Proudly distributed by Publishers Group West®

All Scripture quotations, unless otherwise indicated, are taken from the Holy Bible, New International Version®, NIV®. Copyright ©1973, 1978, 1984, 2011 by Biblica, Inc.™ Used by permission of Zondervan. All rights reserved worldwide. www.zondervan.com The "NIV" and "New International Version" are trademarks registered in the United States Patent and Trademark Office by Biblica, Inc.™

**Morgan James BOGO™**

A **FREE** ebook edition is available for you or a friend with the purchase of this print book.

[ ]

CLEARLY SIGN YOUR NAME ABOVE

**Instructions to claim your free ebook edition:**
1. Visit MorganJamesBOGO.com
2. Sign your name CLEARLY in the space above
3. Complete the form and submit a photo of this entire page
4. You or your friend can download the ebook to your preferred device

ISBN 9781636981994 paperback
ISBN 9781636982007 ebook
Library of Congress Control Number:
2023936098

**Cover & Interior Design by:**
Christopher Kirk
www.GFSstudio.com

Morgan James PUBLISHING
**Builds**
with...
**Habitat for Humanity®** Peninsula and Greater Williamsburg

Morgan James is a proud partner of Habitat for Humanity Peninsula and Greater Williamsburg. Partners in building since 2006.

Get involved today! Visit: www.morgan-james-publishing.com/giving-back

# DEDICATION

*To my five children and my unborn grandson. One of my life's
objectives was to raise my children in a home environment
that, unlike my childhood, didn't involve routine trauma,
but would be the start of generational triumph.
May God bless you and your children's children for generations.*

# TABLE OF CONTENTS

# Acknowledgments

Without my wife, Sheila Qualls, this book would not have been written and my life would be for the worse without her. I met Sheila when she was fifteen-years-old, and we started dating a year or so later. At the time, I didn't have plans to marry her and, obviously, our life together would not have unfolded as it has today. Sheila has enriched my life incalculably, and I thank God for her and how she has blessed our family. People who have had a chance to get know Sheila love and respect her.

To Christian pastors that stand for truth in love and do not shy away from the truth of scripture, thank you. A personal thanks to the pastors of the churches we needed, that, through the truth of scripture and Jesus Christ, changed the course of life and the life of my family for the better: Dr. Joel Stowell; Tony Evans, Oak Cliff Bible Fellowship Church, Dallas, TX; Max Lucado, Oak Hills Church, San Antonio, TX; Doug Thuen, Sparta E-Free Church, Sparta, NJ; Mark Henry, and Revive Church, Brooklyn Park, MN.

There are many men and women, who helped me personally and professionally throughout my life. Some of these people will go unnamed because they prefer to remain anonymous.

To Frank Hunnes for giving me my first job when I left the military and provided strong leadership and coaching while we worked together and friendship after my departure from the company. For all my former colleagues at J&J that helped our family during the severe car accident that was life changing event for us.

To Tim George for his sage-like advice and quiet, determined leadership during tremulous times as two great companies merged and the fallout that followed. Most people don't know the strong character of the man you are.

I want to acknowledge and thank Alice Crider, my writing coach for her help in the production of my first book. She was patient and professional throughout the process. I also want to thank my editor, Sarah Rexford, who took my manuscript through its final edits before production.

# PREFACE

The Prodigal Project: A Hope for American Families, is my story and the series of lessons learned through the formidable years of my life. For readers who are practicing Christians or familiar with Judeo-Christian traditions, the references to God, religious faith, and other concepts will not seem odd or out of place. However, if you are reading this book and consider yourself not religious, you may find it odd how often my personal faith is interwoven throughout the book. This preface is written specifically for you.

We are living through one of the most secular, unchurched, and amoral times in our country's history. Most Gen X'ers (people 37 to 52) and younger wouldn't know that there was a deliberate purging of anything referencing the Bible, the Ten-Commandments, and other Christian concepts out of the public square in America. This purging began in the 1960s and is active to this very day.

To give you a perspective, as a kid growing up in the 1970s, prayer before public school sporting events was the norm. Now it is the exception. It wasn't just Chick-fil-A and Hobby Lobby that were closed on Sundays. Most businesses were closed on Sundays. Even if you were not a religious person, you and your family benefited from this social norm. Over the years, there has been a deliberate campaign to marginalize these former social norms to the far corners of society.

We have a type of government that separates religion from state government. However, the founders of the country knew that this form of government could only function if the people were a moral people. John Adams, the second President of the United States said, "Our Constitution was made only for a moral and religious people. It is wholly inadequate to the government of any other."

As Americans, we voluntarily obeyed the laws because we had a moral compass rooted in the Ten Commandants, the Golden Rule, and other Biblical concepts. Without a moral foundation, more government oversight, intervention, and law enforcement are required. Clay Christensen was a renowned author, Harvard professor, and business consultant. He once said succinctly, "if you take away religion, you cannot hire enough police."

# INTRODUCTION

I was born in 1963 when Black Americans had not yet received full rights per the Civil Rights Act of 1968. Mine was one of the last generations to experience integration busing in elementary school in the 1970s. During that time, approximately 80 percent of Black families had two parents. Divorce and children born out of wedlock were the exception, not the norm. Even the few television shows with Black actors featured two-parent families.

Back then, Black culture was rooted in faith, family, and education. At the time, our heroes were Hank Aaron, Willie Mays, and Dr. King. Our generational family members listened to the music of Aretha Franklin, the Temptations, and Gladys Knight.

We were poor in financial assets, but we grew up with values rich in the moral tradition of Judeo-Christian beliefs. We espoused the same values that every American ethnic group used to uplift themselves: don't steal from others, work hard in school, and respect your elders and authority figures, including teachers and police. My mother and father worked all their lives and expected me and my siblings to work for what we wanted as children, and later, as adults.

As a child, I was unaware that our culture was merging on the path of a crisis. I didn't know about the political agenda to make the Black community dependent on government handouts or the immense level of evil to transform a culture from 80 percent two-parent families to 80 percent fatherless homes—for reasons that have motivated men from the dawn of time: greed for power and money. Why do I believe it was greed for power and money? Because for more than fifty years, there has not been one national initiative to reverse the trend of fatherless homes by the political party that is supposed to "represent" the Black community, by the NAACP, the National Urban League, or the Council of National Black Churches (an organization that represents 80 percent of Black pastors in the United States).

At a young age, I realized I was on a different path than my peers and my siblings—an uncommon path. I didn't know what or who was taking me on a different path. I know now it was God who led me in that direction. As you'll read in the pages ahead, I eventually came face-to-face with my calling: to help heal our country and restore the Black community to faith, family, and education, especially for our children. Essentially, to redeem a culture in crisis.

I spent my adult life working hard, getting an education, and determined to accumulate financial security in the private sector economy. I never wanted to live the life I was exposed to with my divorced mother in Harlem, New York, and then later with my father in a trailer park in Oklahoma. I rose to the level of vice president leading sales and marketing teams for Fortune 100 companies. Starting a nonprofit organization and running for public office was never part of my plans. However, God's plan for our lives doesn't require our prior approval.

At times I've felt like David, up against a giant too big to slay but also determined to behead the beast. That's why I've written this book. I am certain my journey in life, the stories I share, and my leadership example are not meant to benefit only Black Americans but all Americans. I believe Black and White Americans have been misled, intentionally causing strife, confusion, and anger to drive an anti-family, anti-American, and anti-God agenda.

It will require leadership and clear thinking to see through the haze of deception to understand that a back-to-basics movement is needed in the Black community as well as serious consideration across the country. I like to call this movement our "Prodigal Project" named after the parable of the prodigal son told by Jesus Christ (Luke 15:11-31).

Whether you are Black, White, or any other color, we need to learn to drop the superficial ideologies that divide us and unite on the ties that bind us together as fellow Americans, Christians, or both. I invite you to join me on this journey. I'll share the story of how I came to be where I am now, and I'll show you what I've learned and discerned along the way. Ultimately, my goal is to convince you that together we can take charge of our destiny as Americans. My prayer is for you to have courage and to see a purpose for your own life that transcends identity, politics, culture, economic class, and ethnicity.

I'll be the first to admit I don't have all the solutions to the problems we are facing as a nation. The first thing to remember is that we owe it to our parents, grandparents, and ancestors to honor their sacrifices that gave us the life and position we have today. Ultimately, we need to restore a sense of honor and respect toward the teaching of God. For centuries, His wisdom has yielded benefits for all mankind, even those that do not follow him. I am confident if we each wake up to the reality we've been living in and begin to take courageous steps for change, He will lead our country on a path of reconciliation, harmony, and prosperity.

# 1: GHETTO KID, TRAILER TRASH, AND CHILD OF GOD

"Pack your backpack, Kendall. We're going on a bus ride." I never questioned Mom, but I wondered where a bus would take us and why Dad wasn't coming with us.

With the structured world of Fort Campbell, Kentucky, home of the 101st Airborne, behind us, New York City loomed large and dark in contrast as the Greyhound bus rolled into Grand Central Station. Busy people scurried about in every direction. The air was so thick you could wave your hand through it and watch it move, like smoke. Horns honked and I could hear sirens in the distance. It all seemed chaotic to my six-year-old mind.

After exiting the bus, my mother, my four siblings, and I climbed aboard a city bus that would take us to my grandparents' neighborhood in Harlem. The city bus smelled like cheap cigarettes and sweat. I couldn't help but stare at a man in ragged clothing who surely hadn't had a bath in weeks. He began talking to himself, then yelling at other passengers. By now it was almost noon, and my stomach was growling.

"I'm hungry, Mom." I whispered, choking back tears.

"We'll eat lunch at Grandma's," she responded as the bus rolled to a stop. "First we have to walk a little ways to get there."

I felt tiny holding my big sister's hand as we began our trek toward Grandma's apartment in the projects, stepping over and around garbage littering the sidewalk. Skyscrapers stretched overhead, and more traffic sounds bounced off their brick walls. People ambled about without acknowledging our presence until suddenly a tall Black man stepped in front of my mother.

"Gimme your money," he demanded.

My mom took a step back. "Please mister," she pleaded. "I have five children, and this is all the money I have."

Another man appeared from the shadows of a nearby alley. "Lady, he doesn't care if you have five kids or ten. You'd better give him your money."

My mother handed the man a small wad of bills, tears in her eyes and hands trembling. In that moment, watching them rob my mother, I stood amazed that no one was doing anything to help us. I vowed to myself I would never be like those men. In fact, I would eventually grow up to protect people against men like that.

It's fascinating how childhood vows stick with you throughout life.

My thoughts drifted back to the neighborhood on the army base we'd left behind, where backyard barbeques, Motown music, and the sounds of happy families still echoed. All I knew was we were not one of those happy families anymore. I had a feeling there wouldn't be any friendly backyard barbeques in this dangerous city.

Mom was sobbing by the time we arrived at her parents' apartment. Grandad wrapped his arms around her and listened as she spilled out her fears and infuriation.

"It's gonna be okay," he said as her tears soaked the shoulder of his flannel shirt.

I had never met my grandparents, but Grandma welcomed us with open arms from her wheelchair, one side of her face distorted from a recent stroke. My granddad's warm smile made me feel welcome and safe when he turned to greet us kids. I was too young to consider where we would all fit in their tiny apartment or where we would sleep. Somehow, we did figure it out. My little brother and I slept in my mom's bed, and my three older siblings slept in the living room on the couch or the floor.

After several weeks at Grandma and Grandad's, we moved into temporary government housing. You'd think settling into a place of our own would be wonderful, but the tiny hotel-like room on the fifth floor of a run-down complex was horrible. It was furnished like you'd expect an old run-down hotel would be. An old, saggy mattress, stained carpet, torn curtains, and a barely upholstered chair. The carpet smelled of sour milk mixed with pet urine, and the tile on the bathroom floor was peeling.

The walls were so thin we could hear screaming, yelling, arguing, and crying in the next room at all hours of the day and night. We had to lock not only the door but the windows when we went out because thieves would climb the fire escape to break in.

Once they stole our small, portable Black and White television, which was the only furnishing we actually owned.

Despite our horrific living conditions, my mom was determined to make a good life for us kids. At six-years-old, I had no idea what a gargantuan mountain that would be for her to climb. She was on public assistance by then and cleaned animal kennels at a pet store where she was paid under the table so she wouldn't lose her welfare benefits.

After several months, we moved to a two-bedroom apartment on the tenth floor of the projects in Harlem. Back then, public housing projects in major cities across the country were filled with fatherless families, predominately Black families, that could not afford their own home or a nicer apartment. The quality of the neighborhood's tenements had decreased drastically, creating an overcrowded and often hopeless housing situation for Harlem's residents.[1]

Still, Mom did her best to make our new home a safe haven. She made sure our apartment was always Pine-Sol-clean and tidy.

"Just because you live in a place like this doesn't mean you have to live like you're *from* a place like this," she would say. I can still hear the resolve in her voice all these years later.

Although my mother didn't finish high school and was at the bottom rung of society, she didn't equate being poor with moral poverty. She expected us to be well-behaved children, work hard in school, and respect teachers and elders. We were

---

1    https://savingplaces.org/stories/the-experimental-history-behind-the-harlem-river-houses#.YDz8ZZNKigQ

taught a moral code of ethics rooted in the Ten Commandments. Moral poverty is easily learned, especially in single-parent families. You adapt to it because the entire community drifts in that direction. Growing up in Harlem, I recall no fathers and no men providing examples of caring for their families. The neighborhood, the culture, and the system were stacked against what my mother tried to teach her children.

Learning that America is a land of opportunity for everyone, including poor Black Americans like myself, took years of unlearning and then learning truth. Compared to most of my peers, I took an uncommon path. But I am living proof that with God's help, a poverty mindset *can* be unlearned and eradicated in one generation. It requires reframing what we've been taught, willingness to buck the status quo, and social discomfort. But it's possible for all of us, regardless of ethnicity.

## BECOMING HYPERVIGILANT

Going to school in Harlem was almost more dangerous than walking the streets. Students started fights for no reason. Children often act out more when there is no father in the home, and 90 percent of the kids in the projects lived with single mothers. Violence was common, and you never knew by who or from what direction you could be attacked. It's even worse in big cities that don't traditionally operate from an unspoken but commonly held moral compass.

I never picked on another kids. However, I must have been an easy target because other boys often picked on me. I once got into a fight with a boy in my third-grade class. I knocked him down to get him to leave me alone, then I turned around to sit back at my desk.

"Kendall! Watch out!" my teacher shouted from the front of the classroom. I turned just in time to see that kid holding a chair above his head and launching it toward me. With the chair seemingly suspended in mid-air, I ducked. The chair clamored to the floor next to me. Just another ordinary day in elementary school.

Walking home from school every day was scary because of the older kids. A kid from junior high or high school would jump out of an alley or from behind a parked car and attack with no provocation. Sometimes they were hoping to get money, but mostly, they attacked for sport: because they could, because they were bigger than me. My older brothers and my sister went to a different school on a different schedule, so they could never come to my defense.

One summer Saturday, my mom took me and my little brother to the Bronx Zoo, one of the largest zoos in the United States. It stretches across 265 acres of park lands and naturalistic habitats separated by the Bronx River, housing at least 4,000 animals. Our outing was a big deal to us, given Mom's limited budget. I was fascinated by the sights, sounds, and smells of animals I had only read about in school.

At one point as we wandered around the maze of wildlife displays, Mom stopped and said, "Come on, boys. Let's get a souvenir," and she led us into the zoo gift shop. "You can each choose one toy." She smiled, clearly proud of being able to spend a little money on us, which was a rare occurrence.

I chose a plastic telescope, the kind that extends when you pull it out of its case, like you're the captain of a ship. With it, I would be able to see all the animals up close. I carried it with pride as we stepped out of the gift shop and headed toward the gorilla exhibit.

After our bus ride home that afternoon, I walked behind my mom toward our apartment building, still fascinated with what I could see through my telescope. Suddenly, it was no longer in my hand. I stopped walking and stared down the street as an older boy darted off with my new toy. I was so stunned, I stood still without saying a word.

Mom turned around and saw my face. "What's wrong, Kendall? Where is your telescope?"

"That kid grabbed it," I said, pointing in the direction the boy ran. In that moment, it was as if I was observing my life from the outside, like a movie in which everyone around me is an actor. *He didn't really want my telescope,* I thought. *He saw me playing with my toy, and he decided to deprive me of it.* Even at seven-years-old, I was learning to process incidents logically.

Now as an adult looking back on that scene, I can also see that taking a new toy away from a smaller kid must have given that boy a feeling of power. I'm certain he threw my telescope in a ditch somewhere once the power rush was over. After all, what kind of bragging rights would he have for stealing a plastic toy? He didn't want the *thing*. He wanted something that someone valued, even if temporarily.

In an environment like the projects of Harlem, studiousness, meekness, and kindness are not virtues with a lot of currency. People become like mean dogs to make sure the other mean dogs don't come after them. We often heard reports in the news about people pushing others onto the subway tracks, so we learned not to stand too close to the edge. People who feel powerless sometimes do mean and violent things to make themselves feel powerful.

I soon figured out that if you live in the projects, you have to walk like you mean business. Hold your head up. Be on high alert. Notice everything around you. People are always watching. If you look vulnerable, you get jumped. That's how my mom was robbed on our first day in New York, and that's how that guy stole my telescope so easily.

Going anywhere in the big city was like running a gauntlet, only we would never run because that made a person look scared and vulnerable. We had to be hypervigilant about our surroundings and never show fear.

Walking home from school, I never knew what I'd encounter once I got to the public housing project. The elevator in our building didn't work half the time, but walking up ten flights of stairs wasn't what I feared. I feared stepping over and around the heroin junkies who knocked out the light bulbs and sprawled across the landings in the stairwells. My feet made crunching sounds as I walked across broken glass. The smell of urine permeated the stairwell. I held my head high and pretended I wasn't afraid, but I was never sure what I would see or who might try to stop me from getting home.

When my mother opened the door to our apartment, it was like sun beaming through a dark cave. The scent of Pine-Sol and the brightness of Mom's smile confirmed I was safe and loved. Our home was like an oasis in a desert of crime, filth, and despair.

We usually had food to eat, but it was far from nutritious and delicious. Government cheese, powdered eggs, peanut butter sandwiches, and oatmeal were our staples. Once Mom cooked cow tongue, which had the consistency of leather. We kids learned not to complain though, because we could see how hard our mother worked to provide for all of us. Even at a young age, I knew the stress of raising five kids alone was taking a toll on her. The anxiety on her face spoke volumes as she tucked us in bed every night.

God did not intend for women to raise kids alone, yet roughly 80 percent of mothers in the Black community are doing so today. In the late 1960s and early 1970s, it used to be 80 percent two-parent families in the Black community. Wherever you find a community with a high percentage of fatherless homes, you will find a community deep in despair, destruction, and death. This is not unique to Harlem or even America. It is a human condition, not a Black or White or brown condition.

This human condition is worsened in a big city environment like New York, due to the pervasiveness of anonymity. Individuals are not noticed or known in a city. In rural areas, people are often known and held accountable, but in large cities, when someone is accosted, bystanders simply watch and do nothing, protecting themselves and their own anonymity.

That's what happened when my mom was robbed on our first day in Harlem. Nobody helped because my mom was "nobody" to them. Your identity and your humanity are easily lost in a big city, and there is no accountability there because everyone is as anonymous as you are.

No child should have to grow up in an unsafe and uncaring environment, but far too many kids do. It doesn't have to be this way. We don't have to stay where we started out in life, and we can help pull future generations out of poverty and violence with three powerful principles: faith, family, and education.

But first, we must resolve to go after them.

## ESCAPE FROM NEW YORK CITY

Harlem's street culture began to absorb my teenage brother and my two sisters like a desert floor absorbs spilled water deep into its cracks. A five-year gap lay between them and me, so I didn't understand exactly why Mom was often upset with them. I didn't understand the drug-laden landscape into which they were falling.

Over time, Mom's mental and emotional health suffered so much from trying to rescue my older siblings from their destructive choices that she was in and out of the hospital more times than I could count. After three years, her fragile health made it difficult to care for all five of us kids. So, my absentee father traveled to New York to move my younger brother Sheldon and me to a trailer park in Oklahoma to live with him.

I was certain we had upgraded to a much higher economic status when we arrived at Dad's mobile home. Though we still lived in poverty, the change in scenery felt hopeful. Compared to the noisy projects in Harlem, the trailer park was quiet except for Friday nights when the nearby dirt racetrack came alive with wannabe NASCAR drivers.

The feeling of safety from crime gives a person the capacity to focus on their dreams. I began to notice how beautiful the sights and sounds around me were. I could hear crickets chirping outside my bedroom window and see stars twinkling in the night sky. I no longer had to worry about what I would get to eat or who was going to attack me every day. Suddenly, I knew I never wanted to live in the ghetto again. I began to dream of a better life than that.

Even though my living conditions had improved dramatically, my life with Dad was all discipline, all the time. This was a stark contrast to Mom's loving and nurturing ways. Dad was an old-school father who believed children should be seen and not heard. He was never affectionate and never played with me, not even a game of catch in the yard.

He was a drill sergeant in the Army and raised us like mini Army recruits. He inspected our rooms to make sure our beds were made and our dresser drawers neat and orderly. When I misbehaved or did something wrong, it was like Zeus came down with lightning and thunder. When that happened, I worked hard to make sure it didn't happen again.

Along with the big change of moving to Oklahoma, I experienced our nation's first attempts at integrated schools. Change is always difficult because we never know what the future holds. When the school board closed Dunbar Elementary School in Lawton, Oklahoma, and began to bus Black kids to White schools, I didn't know what to expect.

I soon found myself attending B.C. Swinney Elementary, an all-White school. As a result of busing, the school now had one Native American boy and two Black kids, one of which was me. It wasn't a completely bad situation except that I was isolated and separated from my friends at my previous school.

The teacher was polite, and the kids did not treat me poorly. In contrast to my school in Harlem, there were no daily fights.

One day in the boys' bathroom, a student asked, "How does it feel being in an all-White school?"

I shrugged. "Go ask Jim." Jim was the Native American kid. My automatic response was the only thought that came to mind while I was peeing in the urinal.

I missed my mother tremendously when we first moved to Oklahoma. We often talked on the phone late at night because long distance rates were cheaper then.

"How are you doing?" she would ask. "Is your dad treating you nice?"

"Yes, Mom, everything's fine," I would answer. I think I was just as concerned about her wellbeing as she was about mine. One time I told her a joke, and I heard her laugh on the other end of the phone. I can't remember the joke now, but I'll never forget how hard she laughed. I always loved to hear her laugh, and it made me miss her even more.

I hated not only what my father had done to our family by divorcing my mother, but also how uncaring and harsh he was. Had my parents stayed married, my mother's nurturing ways may have taken the edge off my dad's stern nature. Two healthy parents in a home balance each other out, and I sensed the imbalance to a greater degree in my dad's home. The disparity often made me feel lonely. Eventually, I grew to resent my father so much that I planned to change my last name.

By middle school, I learned that I had to forge my destiny on my own somehow. Without my mom to nurture me and show pride in my accomplishments, and with only harsh, over-the-top discipline from my dad, I knew I had to figure out life with very little parental guidance. This is common for children of divorced parents or children that never had a father at all. Unfortunately, these kids make poor choices when they have no one to provide wise counsel. Poverty and fatherlessness have become all too normal in our society, which puts kids at an incredible disadvantage growing up.

Later in life, my older siblings recalled stories about our time together as a family before the divorce. I had no memories of those days because I was so much younger than they were. As we grew into adulthood, we really had no relationship with each other except for the respect and admiration we shared for our mother.

Looking back over my childhood years, I can see how God had His hand on me, though. A curious kid, I once asked Mom where God came from. I didn't know much about Him, but I did believe in His existence.

"Jesus is the Son of God," Mom replied.

"I know about *that guy*, but I want to know where God came from, you know, *the main guy*," I said.

"Well, He was just born," Mom answered.

"You mean like, poof, He was just there?" I asked.

"Something like that, yes." Mom smiled her soft, loving grin I loved so much.

I figured that was all Mom knew, but I was sure there had to be more to God's existence, so, as with so much in life, I decided I would need to learn more about God myself.

Even with my limited understanding of God, I had a sense that He somehow kept me safe amid the depravity and violence I was exposed to. He gave me a loving mom and a protective, though stern, father. Even though I resented my strict dad, that trailer in Oklahoma under the stars felt a lot safer than Harlem.

Along my uncommon path, I would later discover that I am a beloved child of God, not just another statistic of poverty in Black America. I would come to realize that anyone with a disadvantaged past can become a difference-maker and lead a fulfilling life in the United States.

It took me many years, but I eventually discovered that where I came from didn't need to define me, that my identity was defined by God, not pop-culture, or even my skin color. The tattered pieces of my beginnings could be redeemed.

# 2: THE AWAKENING YEARS

E ven as a young child, I knew that with my father in the military, it was only a matter of time before we were relocated to another Army base. We began packing our belongings for a move to Fort Shafter near Honolulu, Hawaii. I imagined surfing, luaus, and humpback whales like I'd seen on a travel poster. I was curious about seeing the ocean for the first time in my life and excited at the opportunity to travel to someplace new. Hawaii sounded like a magnificent adventure.

When we arrived, we were greeted by a transitional family the Army provided to help us adapt to our new surroundings. Mr. and Mrs. Tidd greeted us and showed my father around the Army base, including the elementary school, commissary (military grocery store), and other essential locations. Mrs. Irene Tidd instantly reminded me of Aunt Bea of Mayberry from the 1970s television show, only she had a slight German accent. Their two sons and daughter were friendly toward me, even though they were a few years older. We often crossed paths at sporting events.

After we moved into our house on the base, Mr. and Mrs. Tidd escorted us to the nearest beach. The ocean was mesmerizing. The way the tide rolled toward the shore and embraced the sand on the beach felt as soothing as my mom's last hug. The low rhythmic rumbling of waves was such a contrast to the random din of city traffic on the mainland. I smelled salt water in the air as the white sand enfolded my feet and clung to my skin. I loved everything about it.

During the three years we lived on Oahu, the beaches became a place of unending exploration. I learned to appreciate what I had as opposed to grieving what I couldn't have. I learned to swim, after which I advanced to boogie boarding, then surfing, though I never got as good as the surfer studs of the North Shore. I once attempted to ride one of those giant curling waves and soon found myself choking on saltwater while struggling to pull my swim trunks back on. I figured I'd just watch from then on or stick to the less intimidating waves on the southern shore.

Soon after we arrived in Hawaii, my dad's girlfriend, Blanche, arrived from Oklahoma and became my stepmother. There was no family conversation about it. They simply got married at the courthouse and then she and her son moved into our three-bedroom house with my dad, my brother Sheldon, and me.

From the outside, we probably looked like a typical family with a mom, a dad, and three boys in a house with a banana tree in the back yard. But inside, we were like strangers sharing a youth hostel. My stepbrother was five years my senior and always seemed annoyed with Sheldon and me. The five of us shared some meals but never held family conversations. We didn't participate in activities together and never created any family traditions. We simply existed under the same roof.

I still held internal resentment toward Dad, but kept my thoughts and feelings to myself. When Dad talked to me, it was usually to give orders. "Take out the trash, son." "Clean up your room." He bought me a bicycle, which was great until the chain broke on it and I was delayed getting home one evening.

"You're late," he barked. "What happened?"

"My bike is broken." I pointed toward the chain dangling from the gears.

Dad looked at my bike. "This is easy to fix. Why didn't you fix it? When I was your age, I built my own bike."

I felt the heat of embarrassment and rage spread up my neck and across my face. *Nobody ever taught me how to fix a bike or how to build one, Smarty Pants,* I thought to myself. I didn't dare say anything out loud for fear he would verbally rip my head off. He never said another word about it, and I made sure I was always on time after that, even though I would be on foot until I could figure out how to fix my bike by myself.

My stepmother was never mean, but she was far from the nurturer my mother was. She never showed any affection toward me or Sheldon, but I didn't care. My loyalties remained with my mother, even though our physical distance was now greater than ever.

In time, I learned Blanche had been an only child and had grown up without a father to protect her. Maybe that's why she seemed untrusting and distant. I've heard step-parenting is the hardest job in the world. Mothers naturally love their own children, but it's not always easy to create a bond with someone else's child. I often laid in bed at night wondering what life would have been like if my parents had stayed married.

Sheldon and I shared a bedroom, but he was two years younger, so we ran with different friends and participated on different sports teams. I played football and ran track. Dad came to my football games mainly because he loved to watch football. Even though I was kind of a star player, Dad never showed any pride in me or acknowledged my skills.

I still missed my mom, but we had less frequent communication due to our time zone differences. When it was 9:00 p.m. in New York, it was only 3:00 p.m. in Hawaii, and I was either still in school or at sports practice or games after school. We wrote letters back and forth, mostly sharing our affection for each other.

In one of my letters to her, I wrote I was lonely and felt I didn't have anyone in my life to go to for emotional support. She didn't respond right away, but my older brother visited once and told me Mom had received my letter.

"Mom can't be with you, but I'll always be here for you," he vowed. I had a feeling he would never be able to keep that promise or fill the void in my heart.

Though my home life wasn't *Leave It to Beaver* perfect, I experienced much more joy in Hawaii than I ever did in Harlem. Being surrounded by palm trees, tropical flowers, and ocean breezes was more life-giving than the concrete and sirens in the city. The natural beauty of the island awakened something in me, and I began to understand my happiness was up to me, not my parents or my siblings.

# ISLAND OF DIVERSITY

I attended sixth grade, middle school, and my first year of high school in Hawaii, and I made several lifelong friends there. The students were a beautiful blend of ethnicities from all over the world: Japanese, Filipino, Chinese, Samoan, European, African American, South American, and Caucasian. Since everyone knew our days there would be limited by the military's relocation orders, we wasted no time getting to know each other. Rather than gravitate only toward kids who looked alike, we bonded in other intangible ways. Were they good at sports? Did they make us laugh? What is the quality of their character? Could you trust them?

It's human nature to be drawn toward people who look and talk like we do. Familiarity provides a perception of safety and acceptance. But when you're transplanted into a place of such diversity, you learn that sameness in looks isn't what counts. It's sameness of character.

I felt accepted and loved for who I was for the first time in my life. Not only was that a tremendous life lesson, but I also ended up with friends who remain in touch to this day.

Many of our teachers had Japanese last names and spoke perfect English. They were kind and treated each of us with equal respect. I didn't sense any hyper-sensitivity about race from them in the least. Mrs. Yokoyama had academic standards and expectations for her students, but she was gentle, even though she never let any of us off the hook. In such an amiable setting, I felt zero concern about my safety like I had on the mainland.

The teachers and students on the base were all from different backgrounds. Together, we were like the ingredients and spices that create a perfect culinary dish. I began to see humanity through a different filter in Hawaii, which changed my outlook on life in general. Instead of seeing certain people as safe and good, I began to realize that anyone could be harmless and friendly or mean and dangerous. I only had to give them time to show their true character.

## WILD BOARS, FIRST DATES, AND PAPER ROUTES

One of my favorite adventures in Hawaii included a three-mile trek up a steep mountain and through some woods to a clearing called Waipuka. Waipuka is a series of three ponds that make up a small part of the Kamanaiki stream on the island. The water flows from an underground artesian spring. The first time my friends and I arrived there, the sight of a waterfall cascading over a cliff into a crystal-clear pool below made my heart race. I'd never seen such beauty in nature.

I don't remember how large the pool under the waterfall was in diameter, but cliff diving into it was the coolest thrill. I would scramble to the top of the cliff, hold my breath, then freefall into the fresh water over and over again. The first time was terrifying, but after that I was hooked. It's that way with any risk in life, isn't it? We take steps toward our fear and find out we're both capable of more than we thought and safer than we imagined.

Cliff diving wasn't the only risky part of our Waipuka tropical outings. We carried spears fashioned from branches broken off the Banyan trees on the trail because we never knew if we would encounter a wild boar. The "feral pigs" in the woods were dangerous. A bite or a gore from a tusk could cause serious injury and infection.[2] Fear shadowed the back of my mind, but I felt like a ready warrior with my spear in hand. In Harlem I had to protect myself from street thugs. In Hawaii it was the wild boars. I'll take wild boars any day over devious human beings.

On weekend evenings, I hung out with my friends at the teen club on base where live bands played the popular music of groups like the Eagles and Earth, Wind, and Fire. Sometimes we went to see a movie at the main theater or wandered into the bowling alley to watch the soldiers in the bowling leagues roll strike after explosive strike. The Teen Club was only a couple of miles from our house, a one-level building that was mostly an open area. Because our base was somewhat central on the island, the kids from Pearl Harbor would come in along with the kids from the Air Force Base.

One Saturday night, the teen club hosted a mock *Dating Game* show, and I was selected to participate as one of the three bachelors attempting to win a date with a pretty girl. Diana Benton played the young lady who would interview the guys and ultimately choose one to be her date. Just like in the television game show, the lovely bachelorette sat on one side of the stage and the three hopeful suitors perched on bar stools on the other side of a dividing wall.

---

2    https://www.westhawaiitoday.com/2018/12/03/hawaii-news/problematic-park-pigs/

"Bachelor Number One, what would you do for a lady if it was cold outside on a date?" Diana asked.

I was Bachelor Number One. I rubbed my sweaty palms on my slacks and said, "I would take off my jacket and gently wrap it around her shoulders."

"What is one word that describes your life?" she asked.

"Adventure," I responded. That was the first word that popped into my mind, so I went with it.

After several questions to the other guys and me, Diana made her decision. "Bachelor Number One, I choose you to be my date."

I almost fell off my bar stool. I had never won a contest before, and I wasn't even sure I wanted to win this one. I got over my uncertainty quickly when the announcer told us we won a dinner at an upscale restaurant off base, and we would be escorted there with two other couples in a Rolls Royce limousine. *First class! How did a kid from Harlem get so lucky?*

The evening of our date was not only fun, but it gave me a taste of a lifestyle I never would have seen back in Harlem. I began to wonder how anyone could afford a life above the scarcity zone I was born into. For that matter, could I ever make a living that provided more than the basics? It dawned on me that hard work and determination, not sheer luck, could free me from the past I'd known. First order of business: figure out how to make enough money to support myself and break free from poverty's constraints.

My first real job was with the *Honolulu Star* newspaper. Even though I had to walk my route because my bike was broken, I loved getting a paycheck for delivering papers. I even had an employee, Sheldon, whom I paid to help me on Sundays because the newspaper was so heavy with advertisements that day. On the Sundays when he chose not to help me, I would have to walk back and forth between my house and my route at least three or four times.

As hard as lugging that heavy shoulder bag was, it seemed worth the effort to earn money on my own. There's a sense of accomplishment and satisfaction in realizing it's possible to be self-sufficient. I'm not sure I'd ever considered that as a possibility during my years in Harlem or when living in Oklahoma. Earning my own way gave me the confidence to believe I would never have to live on government assistance like my mother and my older siblings.

## BACK TO THE MAINLAND

Hawaii was like a giant slice of happiness pie, and I hated the thought of leaving my friends and going back to the mainland. Oklahoma had saved me physically from the ravages of Harlem, but Hawaii and the friends I made soothed my soul and set my spirit free. The day we left, my friends followed us to the airport and placed leis around my neck. The flowers piled up so high they covered my ears.

Meanwhile Dad was yelling, "Kendall, hurry up! We'll miss our flight!"

As much as I resisted leaving Hawaii, I did have one thing to look forward to. I would get to visit Mom in New York. The first summer after we returned, and every summer throughout high school, I traveled via Greyhound bus to stay with her for two weeks. We took long walks through Central Park and she listened to my stories about Hawaii and high school. She laughed at my jokes, and often said, "I'm proud of you, son." I reveled in our conversations because Mom was my only family member to express loving kindness toward me.

When it was time for me to leave for the bus station, Mom would always hug me, then she would pull back with her hands on my shoulders, look me in the eye, and say, "I love you. And remember, God loves you." Departing was sad. I knew she truly cared about my wellbeing and my future, but our time together was so limited.

Upon returning to Fort Sill Army base near Lawton, Oklahoma, Dad was promoted to Master Sergeant. Blanche worked in the Post Exchange, which afforded us a typical, American, middle-class life. Since Dad didn't pay child support to my mother anymore, he and Blanche were able to buy a house in Lawton. When we moved into our three-bedroom, one-and-a-half bath new construction track home, we were one of three Black families on the street. I still shared a room with Sheldon, which I didn't mind because at least we weren't living in a trailer park again.

Not much had changed in Lawton schools while I was away except my peers had grown taller and physically stronger. Eisenhower High School was integrated with about a third of the students Black and the remainder White. There was no racial tension to speak of, only informal boundaries among certain cliques. The Black students readily accepted me, so I mostly hung out with them as I settled into my new school schedule. Still, I missed the colorful diversity and the acceptance I experienced in Hawaii.

Watching the athletic prowess of some of my classmates, I realized I wasn't going to be a football star in my new school. I had been a decent athlete in Hawaii, but it became clear I would not be able to compete like that in Oklahoma. I participated in track and field, as well as cross country, however, I wasn't competitive at a state level. I turned my attention to academics and got serious about being a good student instead.

I also joined junior ROTC, Reserve Officers Training Corps, in high school. I liked the emphasis on citizenship, character and leadership development, and community service. I excelled in all of it, which made me favorably inclined to start a military career.

When I would come home from school, nobody ever asked, "Are you doing your homework?" or, "How was ROTC this week?" My dad and stepmom never checked up on my progress, so I figured it was all up to me. I knew that once I finished high school, I could decide to do whatever I wanted with my life. We also didn't discuss college or how to prepare for it, but that motivated me to start planning my own way.

We weren't living in poverty anymore, but Dad had us on a tight budget. He was a child of the Great Depression and believed in doing everything from scratch. He was an accomplished DIYer long before it was socially trendy to be one.

"You know, if you have a house, you need a pickup truck because you'll have to haul materials for repairs and remodeling," he said. He bought a small pickup and parked it on the street because we were unable to fit two cars in the driveway. Then he began converting our garage into a den.

Sheldon and I were drafted to help with the remodeling project. Dad decided we needed a wider driveway since we would no longer have a garage in which to park our car. This meant we first had to dig the trench for a new driveway, then pour cement to pave it. Dad insisted that we mix our own cement from raw materials. If you've ever tried to stir gravel, sand, and water together in a giant bucket, you know how back-breaking it is.

Dad also decided we would do all our car maintenance ourselves. When the transmission fell out of my first car, he said, "It's too expensive to buy a new transmission from a repair shop. You'll have to fix it yourself."

I don't mind strenuous work, but strenuous work that I'm not good at in one-hundred-degree humid weather was another motivator to go to college. I admire anyone who chooses a career in the trades or does physical labor, but it wasn't an interest of mine, and I would not be good at the work if I pursued it as a career. I became more determined than ever to excel in school.

Our childhood and young adult experiences often give us clues as to how we'll live our lives as adults. Sometimes it's easy to go along with whatever life hands us. I could have thought, *this is how life is. Just do what everyone else is doing.* That would have taken me down a completely different road than the one I took. Instead, I thought, *there must be another way to live.*

For all I know, God may have heard my thoughts as a prayer and begun leading me toward my future.

# God's Guiding Hand

While I was busy studying, running track, and working part-time at a veterinary clinic cleaning dog cages to make money for college, the Lord was busy orchestrating a different aspect of my future.

One day during my junior year of high school, my buddy Cedric, who was a senior, asked me for a favor. "You know that pretty sophomore girl, Sheila Rogers?" Cedric said. "I want to ask her to the prom, but I'm nervous. Would you ask her for me?"

Guys are so timid sometimes, but I didn't have anything to lose by helping my friend, so I went looking for the girl.

Sheila and I were already casual friends, so I had no problem approaching her. I could easily see why Cedric was attracted to her. Sheila was gorgeous and different than other girls. She didn't hide her beautiful skin with an abundance of makeup, and her imperfect, cute nose made her look kind of like Barbara Streisand. I knew she had spirit and spunk because she played basketball and cheered on the pom-pom team.

Setting aside my own attraction to her, I fulfilled my promise to Cedric and told her he would like to escort her to the senior prom.

"That's nice, but no, thank you," Sheila replied. Her brown eyes were soft but determined, and she was quite sure of her response.

"Aww, come on," I urged. "Cedric is a great guy. He tells funny jokes and drives his own car! You'll have a blast if you go with him." I figured I had to try my best for my friend, even though I was secretly glad she said no.

When she declined again, despite my efforts to persuade her, I said, "Well, since you're free for the prom, how would you like to go with me?"

"Yes." She smiled without hesitation, her eyes sparkled, and my heart melted. I wasn't sure if Cedric would ever forgive me, but I couldn't let that sway me.

We had a wonderful time bopping to the music of Michael Jackson, Prince, and Journey. When the DJ called for our first slow dance, I noticed I had come a long way since my first slow dance in sixth grade wtih Nora Harrington. I had shifted stiff-legged, side-to-side, holding Nora's elbows as Barry Manilow's song "Mandy" played on the speakers in the school gym.

Dancing with Sheila was a brand-new experience. I wanted to hold her close, to smell her perfume, to feel her breath on my neck. I had dated a few other girls before, but none of them even came close to the way Sheila moved my heart. We began spending a lot of time together after that dance. One day I told her a silly joke about the scar on my neck that made her laugh. She later told me that's when she decided to keep me.

Years later, after we were married and had children, I instructed my sons on how to win a woman's heart. First is to use your jacket, sport coat, or a blanket to keep her warm. Women always seem to be cold. The second is non-sexual hugs, and the clencher is to make them laugh. Have a sense of humor.

## CONTRAST AND CLARITY

I started spending after-school and weekend time at Sheila's house. I relished her company, and her family made me feel welcome. Sheila often invited me to church. I liked going, not necessarily because of the preaching, which was usually boring, but mostly so I could be with Sheila.

Sheila's parents, Mr. and Mrs. Rogers, sat in a pew close to the front of the church, and we sat directly behind them. I enjoyed the singing and marveled at how Mrs. Rogers stood tall and belted out every hymn like she was on stage at Carnegie Hall. Church usually ended around 2:00 p.m., after which we all went back to their house for an early supper.

Though I wasn't intentionally seeking God at the time, I believe I was unconsciously basking in His presence. The principles and precepts I picked up by osmosis would serve as building blocks for my life in years to come.

As early as Monday during the school week, I began looking forward to the next Sunday and more time with Sheila. Dad, on the other hand, wasn't keen about losing his weekend home improvement labor. I came home one Sunday evening to find him fuming.

"Where have you been? I've been looking for you for hours!" he shouted.

"I went to church and stayed for supper with Sheila's family," I said.

He became angry. He grabbed my arm and held his other hand in a fist as if he was going to hit me, which he had never done before. It scared me so much that I ran to my room and slammed the door. *Why couldn't we have been a family like Sheila's?* The contrast between our two homes broke my heart.

As soon as I heard my dad leave the house, I emptied my room of everything I could fit in my car and drove away. I moved in with a friend and never told Dad I wasn't coming home. Two weeks later, he tracked me down and asked why I left.

"It's time for me to move on," I answered.

He shook his head and walked away without another word. It would be years before we ever spoke to one another again.

During my senior year of high school, I thought I would go to college and major in criminal justice. I wanted to become a police officer so I could protect the community from men that terrorized women and children like those in my old neighborhood in Harlem. I soon became a first-generation college student. However, I had little preparation for the rigors of academic performance at the collegiate level. Regardless, I chose to enroll in a small state college in southern Oklahoma, which was just right for me. If I had attended the larger state university or a private college like Rice University or Emory, I would have failed miserably. I didn't realize it at the time, but decades later, I was diagnosed with dyslexia.

Before Sheldon graduated from high school, he moved out and got an apartment with his girlfriend. He eventually married his girlfriend, worked full time at a pizza delivery shop, and later became the manager. Sadly, his life crumbled when he got a divorce and moved back to New York City.

Until then, Sheldon and I had always been together. We experienced the same terrors in New York, the same racial tensions in Oklahoma, and the same wonderful experiences in Hawaii. We had shared the same lack of emotional support from weakened family bonds. Though Sheldon and I also had the same opportunities in life, we took dramatically different paths into adulthood. Our biggest difference was how we chose to view hard things in life.

It's a mistake to think difficult experiences are bad. When we encounter something we don't like, mixing and pouring cement in sweltering heat, we may think we're being tested or punished, but we're not. We're being given an opportunity to see the contrast that clarifies our preferences and shines a light on our true desires. It doesn't have to feel like something is going wrong. Instead, we can believe something is going right. Yet all too often, we obsess over what we don't like, and it blinds us to better opportunities.

Railing against what we don't want will become a sure path to self-destruction. Instead, we need to explore what the disparity may be pointing toward.

Living with my dad helped clarify what I didn't want and helped me begin a search for what I truly desired. Watching my peers and siblings make poor life choices helped me see what would not be good for me, which pointed me toward a life I would thrive in.

Contrast helps us clarify. We may never know more clearly what we do want than when we experience what we don't. If we notice what we like and don't like, what drains and energizes us, or what we're good or not good at, we can see more options than we previously imagined. Being introspective when we encounter potential life choices can motivate us to choose a direction that best suits us.

I could have complained about all the times I was uprooted and moved throughout my childhood. I could have wrecked my life out of anger toward my dad. Or I could look for what I wanted instead.

By the time I graduated from high school, I was determined to search for a different life.

# 3: IN SEARCH OF A DIFFERENT LIFE

To help pay my college tuition, I enlisted in the Army Reserve in 1981 just before I graduated from high school. I attended basic training at the age of seventeen (with parental consent) in Fort Knox, Kentucky, in June of that year. Sheila and I wrote letters to each other, and she sent homemade cookies to me at boot camp. I performed well and was selected to be a squad leader even though most of the men were at least five years my senior. It was challenging, but it built my confidence intellectually as well as physically.

After two years of full-time school and military service, I got a break and took Sheila to New York to visit my mother. In 1983, the city's reputation for crime and disorder was still very apparent, and I felt responsible for Sheila's safety. I was on high alert every time we went out sightseeing, watching over my shoulder for potential danger.

Additionally, I had a sense that Mom was checking her out, looking for character flaws and wondering if Sheila was right for me.

One morning before leaving to tour the city, I pulled out Mom's ironing board to press the shirt I wanted to wear. Sheila asked if I would iron her blouse as well, so she could finish doing her hair.

When Mom saw me ironing, she slid up next to me and murmured, "You shouldn't be ironing her clothes. She should be ironing yours."

I chuckled and kept ironing. "It's okay. Times are changing, Mom."

"Don't let her take advantage of you." Mom wagged an arthritic finger in my face. She wasn't about to let anyone misuse her little boy. But Mom was polite and cordial toward Sheila, even as she sized her up. She knew I loved Shelia and wanted us to be happy.

Before we arrived, Mom saved up enough money to buy the two of us tickets to *Chorus Line*, the longest running show on Broadway in the 1980s. The storyline seemed appropriate for that time in my life since I, too, was looking for a place to fit into the world. I was beginning to see that even the smallest details were contributing to an overarching, God-designed plan, even if I couldn't yet see all the puzzle pieces aligned.

As Sheila and I prepared to leave New York, Mom hugged each of us, then grasped my hands in hers. "I love you," she said. "I'm proud of you." I fought back tears as my heart swelled with gratitude and love. I never heard those words from my father, and it meant so much to hear them from my mom. Sadly, that was the last time I would see my mom.

When Sheila and I got married in 1986, I offered to pay for Mom's flight, but she refused to come to our wedding. Knowing Dad and his wife would be at the ceremony, she didn't want to make it awkward for me. I was sad, yet I understood her discomfort.

We continued to talk on the phone regularly over the next two years, but due to my military obligations I wasn't able to visit her like I had before. Mom called one evening in 1988 to ask if she could come live with Sheila and me. The burden of city life had taken a toll on her emotionally. She was always on guard and feeling stressed by all the noise and relentless drama. The biggest weight on her heart and soul was she had seen three of my siblings in serious trouble many times. My older brother and sister were incarcerated for drug-related crimes, and now the baby in our family was going to jail as well. Her heart was broken, and Mom became clinically depressed.

When our children's lives take a turn in the wrong direction, we as parents feel responsible no matter how old the child is. But it seems we especially want to protect the youngest child. Maybe this is because their DNA is likely to go the farthest into the future, carrying part of us with them. Perhaps that's why the baby of the family often receives the most affection from parents.

Mom had originally given birth to eight kids, but only five lived beyond infancy. Now three out of five were behind bars. Her parents had died a few years earlier. She didn't have any close friends in New York. She was in utter despair. Hopeless and alone.

I felt terrible. Mom had nowhere to turn in her depression. I wanted to bring her to a place of emotional safety, but I had orders to go to South Korea, not to mention a new wife. At the time, an assignment in South Korea was a duty station that was considered so hazardous that soldiers had to leave their families stateside. The logistics and timing didn't work. It would not have worked out to leave my mother and my new wife alone while I was deployed for a year. They hardly knew each other, so it didn't seem fair to Sheila or good for Mom.

"I can't make that work right now, Mom. We'd love to have you come after I get back from Korea."

"I understand." Her voice trembled.

"I love you, Mom," I said.

"I love you, too, son." That was the last time I heard my mother's voice.

Two days later, my dad showed up at my house.

"I need to talk to you," Dad said as he stepped through the front door and into my living room.

We had begun talking again after I moved out during the summer following my senior year of high school, but we never discussed the tension between us. We had just smoothed it all over and kept going as if nothing ever happened. We had a cordial relationship and talked occasionally. We discussed politics, unfair taxes, etc., but never mentioned the past, the family, or anything personal.

Now, Dad turned to face me. "Your mother is gone. She jumped off the roof of her fifteen-story apartment building. She died instantly."

He continued saying something about Mom's emotional and mental instability, trying to offer words of sympathy, but I couldn't hear him. It was like someone put earmuffs on my head, making everything sound muffled. My heart pounded in my ears. I blamed my dad for most of what had happened in our family, but in that moment, I blamed myself for my mother's death.

I wanted to shout at him. To tell him it couldn't be true, but I knew in my gut it was. Instead, I just stared at Dad, numb with shock as he slowly turned and left. It seemed like another fallen domino in our crumbled family structure.

A moment later, I felt Sheila's hand on my arm. When I turned toward her, she wrapped her arms around me and cried. I was numb. Couldn't cry. Sheila cried *for* me.

The weight of guilt lay heavy on my shoulders, and still does in some ways. Was I responsible for Mom's death because I didn't let her come live with us? Would that have made a difference? Enough of a difference?

Regrets in life are stifling, especially if we cannot change a situation. In time I knew I had to forgive myself so guilt couldn't trigger chronic stress.

When Sheila's father learned of my mother's death, he insisted on paying for a round trip ticket to New York so I could attend her funeral. The church was packed with aunts, uncles, cousins, and neighbors from the projects. Moments before the service began, a van pulled up, and my three siblings appeared in prison garb and ankle chains, escorted by an armed guard. My heart ached when the officer informed the family that we were not allowed to embrace them. Their grief was evident on their faces, but none of them spoke about it.

After Mom's funeral, everyone gathered in the reception hall. My aunts and cousins all said they were happy to see me doing well as a college graduate now serving in the Army. Their accolades were affirming in the moment, but deep inside I felt distraught at how shattered my family was. I was aware of a mixture of regret for not being there for Mom and a motivation to do even more after seeing my siblings in chains.

## GRIEF AND REGRET

It took me twenty years to fully grieve Mom's death. I didn't cry right away or even at her funeral. I carried my pain internally and compartmentalized it for a long time. I have quietly grieved my death of my mother in slow drips of occasional tears for thirty years, much like the *USS Arizona* that has been dripping oil slowly for more than eighty years since the Pearl Harbor attack in WWII.[3] I could only let the pressure out slowly over time because I believed releasing my grief all at once would have consumed me. It may not have been the best approach to handling grief.

In retrospect, I should have sought professional counseling. However, for a guy who started life in the ghetto of Harlem and

---

3    https://www.civilbeat.org/2020/02/oil-constantly-leaks-from-the-uss-arizona-is-that-an-environmental-problem/#:~:text=The%20USS%20Arizona%20had%20just,two%20days%20after%20the%20attack.&text=It's%20believed%20between%202014%2C000%20and,to%20leak%20for%20500%20years.

upgraded to a trailer park in Oklahoma, I managed it the best way I knew how.

Grief has no middle and sometimes no end. It can sneak up at random times, reminding us of what we once had. Similarly, the pain of regret can result in refocusing and taking corrective action or pursuing a new path. The tragedy of my mother's life motivated me to make a difference in my own life and in the lives of children in the Black community. When I think of impoverished single Black mothers with all their kids, I feel compassion for them. I am passionate about freeing them and their fatherless kids from the cyclical poverty they live in.

*I'll never leave my wife with the burden of the world on her shoulders and the tiny shoulders of our children,* I vowed to myself. I was determined to never let my future family with Sheila crumble as my family of origin had. I knew I must continue to move forward and toward a better life, and a life worth living requires one step *in the right direction* at a time.

## THE HIGH PRICE OF ADDICTION

When I spoke with my younger brother on the phone after he was arrested, he was angry because Dad didn't want to pay for an attorney.

"Why do you need an attorney?" I asked.

"A lawyer can help reduce the sentence," he argued.

I made no comment and only processed what I heard. My brother was terrified of being locked up and his only thoughts were about getting out as soon as possible, not about what he did to get himself there in the first place. He just wanted to be rescued. He didn't want to face the consequences of his own actions. Because he couldn't pay for his own release, and our dad wouldn't bail him out, he spent three years behind bars.

Many poor people turn to drugs to numb their despair. Some turn to drugs for "easy" money. My brother did both, and it cost him dearly. He died several years later from HIV due to using dirty needles for his heroin addiction.

Being poor doesn't necessarily cause drug addiction, but poverty or a poverty mindset increases stress and feelings of hopelessness. It decreases self-esteem, social support, and access to healthcare.[4]

After my older brother was released from prison, he moved to Philadelphia where he married a woman who had children. They later had a child together. Unfortunately, they ended up divorced, and my brother eventually moved to suburban Atlanta without his family.

My sister also spent a few years in prison. She had four children from three different men. I find it sad that our government subsidized women to have children out of wedlock and provided even more money to remain unmarried. That certainly didn't seem to work in favor of women or the children.

My other older sister died from complications of diabetes.

Seeing what addiction did to each of my siblings motivated my desire to restore two-parent families as the standard for the Black community. In my opinion, it is the fastest way to eradicate poverty and improve academic achievement.

---

4    https://stjosephinstitute.com/understanding-the-relationship-between-poverty-and-addiction/

Despite being born into, and growing up in, the same culture, despite having my childhood roots in the same atmosphere of poverty and despair, I am the only one in my family to have broken away from the cultural influences we all knew. I had the honor of finding a loving spouse who influenced me toward faith in God. This became my guidance system. I discovered that God's prescription for life is not a restriction but it's to help us avoid the misery, the pain, and the hurt of making poor choices.

And by His grace, I was shown the difference between making decisions that lead to life rather than those that lead to death. I chose life.

## FROM ARMY TO PRIVATE SECTOR

As I mentioned earlier, I spent four years in the Army Reserve while I was in college in Oklahoma, and four years afterward on active duty as an artillery officer at Fort Sill, Oklahoma. I was then sent to the DMZ (demilitarized zone) in South Korea on that one year "unaccompanied" tour, which meant I couldn't bring Sheila with me.

The Korean war had stopped decades earlier in a ceasefire, but the conflict was never declared over. It was still considered an active military campaign because the violence could flare up unexpectedly.

As my tour of duty came to an end, I began weighing my options for work beyond the Army. Nobody in my family had ever worked in the private sector. Dad and other family members said it was a bad idea to attempt to work in private businesses. Their perspective of the civilian world was tainted by their experience of growing up and living in the Jim Crow south where Black people couldn't participate in the free enterprise market.

"You can't trust people in private business," they said.

"You can't expect fairness from White business owners."

"The military is the only place to be treated equally and to get a fair shot for promotions based on your merit."

I understood their concerns, but I didn't want to spend my life in the military. I saw how frequently my dad was away from our family with constant relocations across the country. I wanted a more stable life for my family and to be present in the lives of my children.

I wanted to be prepared to work in the private sector, so I obtained a liberal arts master's degree in communications.

When I talked to an executive recruiter about getting prepared for the civilian market, he said, "Your master's degree is great, but a business-related graduate degree would be better." So, I went back and earned a master's in economics. Twenty years later, I went back to school and earned an MBA from the University of Michigan, a top 10 Business School.

When asked why I worked toward so many degrees, my answer is, "Leaders are constant learners. We need to be prepared for market shifts, world changes. We need to be able to speak the language, be effective, and deploy new types of analysis into our business and the problems we face. It's really to stay on top of the game."

When I speak of the importance of education, I don't mean higher institutional learning exclusively. I mean all-inclusive, hands-on training in the trades as well. I don't like that people look down on "blue collar workers" as if they are uneducated and therefore unintelligent. I cringe when I hear someone say, "Hey, if you don't go to college, you're going to be stuck in a trade." There are a lot of people who don't want to work in an office. They want to work with their hands, and God bless them. We need people like that.

We need people to build our buildings, improve our roads, and create beautiful craftsmanship and art. These people are just as important in our society as the person who becomes an accountant or a CEO. Many of them are more financially stable than college-educated professionals working in a cubicle in a big corporation. They often become entrepreneurs who have houses on a lake or in the mountains because they've been educating themselves for a long time. They're the backbone of this country.

When I say education, I'm talking about how you improve yourself to be a benefit to society and to provide for your family.

I often joke that I didn't need any of those degrees because I already had a PhD—I was Poor, Hungry, and Determined. I had an internal motivation to succeed. From my perspective, a fire in the belly is required for one to be successful. It doesn't matter if we get a college education or hands-on training in a trade. What matters is our ambition and vision for our life.

I began work with Johnson & Johnson in 1990, and I enjoyed that industry. The private sector has a way of educating people. After a period of training, I began my career in sales, then in sales management. Later, I was promoted to the home office where I was responsible for marketing an anti-infective in the hospital market.

I share this to show that acquiring education or special training will always benefit people with a desire to learn. People with good academic and educational backgrounds tend to get well-paid jobs. Generally speaking, the higher their education and accomplishments, the better their employment options. Additionally, people who educate themselves have a high probability of transforming their lives, thus contributing to a decrease in society's poverty rates.

My personal and professional career was not a solo performance. Many people, Black and White, rich and poor, male and female, helped me along the way personally and professionally. This truth underscores another concept important to our quest of making a difference, no matter where we started.

## UNEXPECTED OUTCOMES

After I finished college and my service in the Army ended, people back in Lawton often said, "You know, yor father is proud of you." They never expected me to turn out the way I did. Nobody ever thought I would stay married or grow up to amount to anything. Though Dad never said he was proud of me to my face, he did show it in other ways. For that I am grateful.

Years later, Dad confided his concerns about all my siblings' problems. I would stop by for a quick visit to say hello when I was in town, and Dad would follow me out to the driveway afterward because he didn't want to talk about his own children in front of my stepmother.

Sometimes we'd be in the driveway for an hour while he poured out his worries about my siblings. I would simply listen, sitting in my car with the window rolled down. I didn't mind taking the time. His kids' lives and how life turned out for them were a heavy burden on his heart. It was clear he had no one else to talk to, so I became that refuge, a coach, or a counselor of sorts.

Looking back, it's simple to see that each of my siblings reached for something other than faith, family, and education. I sometimes wonder what their lives would have been like had they grasped those principles early on. But like so many others born into poverty and despair, who believe they had no other options, that what they were handed dictated what and who they would become, they each chose paths that wrecked their lives.

Many people overlook the idea of exploring a life outside of the one they're born into. It's easy to listen to negative people who inadvertently keep us stuck in a rut. Becoming a victim seems appropriate because so many people say we are. The difficult step is to try something different, read something different, and believe something different. Taking responsibility for our choices, making one right decision after another even when they're risky, adopting faith in God, and searching for a different life can not only be our greatest adventure, but lead us to a life we didn't dream possible.

# 4: JUST BECAUSE YOU CAN DOESN'T MEAN YOU SHOULD

I t has been said that the measure of a man is not how well he handles adversity but how well he handles success. When things are going well, pride can sneak in, and the decisions we make can be detrimental to our futures.

After college, I served on active duty for several months as a new second lieutenant in the United States Army. I was driving an MGB convertible, earning good money, and feeling oh, so confident about myself and how far I'd progressed in my life. Perhaps I was a little too confident, bordering on full-blown pride. As we all know, "pride goes before a fall," and I was about to dive headlong into it.

Sheila and I had been dating since high school, and by then she was finishing her senior year of college. She had opted to attend the same school I went to so we could be close enough to continue our relationship, even though she had been accepted to a university with a higher reputation and collegiate ranking.

I finally paid off an engagement ring I had on layaway at Zales for six months. I know, it's the K-Mart of fine jewelry, but it was the best I could do at the time. The one-third karat diamond was barely visible, but I was proud of myself for making a purchase that no man in my family had ever done.

I had "the talk" with Sheila's father, who said yes and told me he already thought of me as a member of his family.

"You've come a long way since you were a pizza boy," he said as he grinned and slapped me on the back.

My proposal to Sheila wasn't any flashier than the ring, but she said yes, and we were engaged to be married in May with invitations sent to hold the date.

It all seemed picture perfect until temptation came calling. I noticed I was getting a lot more attention from girls than I had received as a poor college kid delivering pizzas to pay for school. I wrestled with thoughts of "sowing my wild oats" until the selfish, prideful side of me won the inner battle, and I called off the wedding. Like a coward, I did it over the phone. It's a good thing we didn't have cell phones back then because I probably would have done the unforgivable and texted her.

Sheila was quiet for a long time on the other end of the phone. "Why now?" she asked. "We have the wedding date set."

"I think it's better to do it now than get a divorce after we're married," I reasoned. I felt terrible, but in my prideful mind I thought claiming I wanted to "explore if marriage is the right thing" for myself sounded acceptable. It's amazing how the brain can develop a rational explanation for the most selfish and mean things we do in life. It didn't even occur to me that breaking Sheila's heart could also break mine.

Because I didn't receive loving affection and attention in my home growing up, any positive affirmation or personal attention was like dopamine to my brain. Unconsciously, I craved love and affection because I didn't receive much from my father, and my mother was too far away to provide it. Although I wasn't seeking it, I found that my new position was generating a lot of interest from the opposite sex. Even though Sheila had already given me her heart and unconditional devotion, the validation was like a powerful magnet pulling me in.

After spending a few months with the party crowd on the weekends and flirting with the hook-up scene, a friend noticed I was exchanging inviting looks with a young lady.

"Kendall, you are with a different woman every weekend," he stated, shaking his head. "You'll never know when the right woman comes along." To this very day, I cannot recall the guy's name or even what he looked like, but his words pierced my heart, and I've never forgotten what he said.

I didn't exactly date anyone. Instead, I engaged in a series of flirtatious relationships and some empty and meaningless one-night stands. Hollywood glamorizes that kind of lifestyle and makes it appear so innocent and harmless. I was drawn in by the feeling of attention, believing I was special to someone new. In retrospect, I realize I was trying to fill a void from my past. I ate up the admiration, not realizing Sheila was right there, loving me for who I am, imperfections and all.

After that guy called me out, I don't know if it was self-talk or God talking, but deep inside I knew the right woman had already come along. I needed to go get her before it was too late. I knew I had to humble myself and hope she would forgive me after I had shattered her heart and dreams. I had made a huge mistake that could have cost me a wonderful future.

I was afraid Sheila wouldn't speak to me, so I asked a friend to call her the next day, then hand me the phone after she answered. The tone of her voice let me know she wasn't happy to hear from me. She felt hurt and confused, but after a few minutes of me groveling, she agreed to let me see her after work that day.

Consequently, I spent weeks and months apologizing to Sheila, hoping to win her trust back. I also apologized to both of her parents and her younger brother. They were all skeptical. I admitted I am human and have many flaws. I acknowledged how much I had hurt her and her family. I had to acknowledge I was a selfish jerk. What I did was wrong. I broke Sheila's heart and I let her parents down. I knew cleaning up the mess I made was the right thing to do, so I was willing to grovel. I was willing to make the effort to do whatever it would take to get her back.

In one conversation I said, "Sheila, if I didn't want you, it would be easy to move on and never approach you or your family ever again. But you're the right one for me, and I don't want to lose you. Eventually, you'll have to marry me because I won't go away."

After three months, she finally believed me. I proposed again, and much to my delight, she said yes for the second time.

I knew she was the only woman for me, and I wanted her in my life forever. We have had our ups and downs in thirty-six years of marriage, but I do not regret groveling, pleading, and doing everything I could to win her heart again.

Years later, Sheila told me she cried in her mom's arms after I called off our wedding. My actions were humiliating for her. In her words, here's what she experienced:

*My first thought was he doesn't really mean it. I tried the song and dance routine to get him back. When it sunk in that he was serious about his decision, I had to deal with the embarrassment of telling people we weren't going to get married. I felt heartbroken, crushed, shocked. The emotional trauma was akin to PTSD, and I didn't know how to deal with it. I was so depressed I stopped going to my college classes. I cried every day for weeks. Months passed, and I thought I would never meet another Mr. Right.*

*When Kendall called, my heart skipped a beat, and waves of caution flooded over me at the same time. After listening to his apologies for several minutes, I said, "Let me think about it... Okay." I agreed to see him later that day. When we met, he asked if I would take him back. I could tell he was truly sorry, but I still felt cautious, so I played hard to get. I kind of wanted to pay him back for his mistake. After three months, I finally felt safe enough to say yes to his second proposal.*

*On our wedding day, Kendall was delayed getting to the church. Nobody told me because they thought he might not show up. I would have been a wreck had I known he was late.*

Having realized how deeply I had wounded Sheila's heart, I learned the hard way the importance of thinking before acting impulsively.

I realized that just because you can do something doesn't mean you should. You can "sow your wild oats" in your youth, but that doesn't mean you should. You can get a divorce, but that doesn't mean you should, because you will take your problems with you. Just because people who came before you did things a certain way or made poor choices, doesn't mean you should do the same. As human beings with free will, there are many choices we can make in life, but that doesn't mean every choice available is good for us or the people close to us.

Americans seem to be so self-centered that we have lost our filter for what's appropriate. We seem to have no deference for others. We tend to be oblivious to people, easily overlooking the needs and desires of those around us.

I rationalized my behavior and convinced myself I was making a good choice to call off my wedding. The human mind can justify any behavior, especially in times of prosperity. The men who flew the planes into the twin towers on 9/11 thought they were doing good. Even Hitler had a rationalization for killing millions of innocent people.

Regardless of my rationalizing, it didn't make my decision right.

## THINK BEFORE YOU ACT

Years ago, I applied for a promotion that I believed I truly deserved, but I wasn't selected for the position. I knew I was more qualified and had more experience than the guy who was hired for the job. I felt bitter and resentful for nearly a year. Out of pride, I wanted to argue with whoever made the decision to pass me over. In fact, I seriously considered claiming racial discrimination. But our first thoughts are usually not our best thoughts.

The Bible instructs Christians to "humble yourselves before the Lord, and he will lift you up" (James 4:10). That's often easier said than done, but I chose to accept the company's decision.

When I finally built up a relationship with my boss enough to ask him what happened, he revealed that he had specifically wanted me on his team. He felt I was what he needed to help turn around the business in the Midwest region. He also told me the other position, although it came with a higher title, was in the same pay scale as the job I was selected for.

The promotion would have required me to relocate my family to San Francisco, which would have been difficult for a family with five kids. Sadly, the guy who got the position, along with everyone who was part of the merger with the legacy company (my company) who relocated to San Francisco faced calamity within six months of relocating. Others were let go, fired, or downgraded in title and responsibility. That would have been my fate had I been selected for the job I wanted.

Not getting that position felt humiliating at the time, but the move would have been detrimental for my family and even more devastating than not being promoted. Subsequently, I did well in the position I was selected for, and the company paid the $100,000 tuition toward my MBA that I obtained from a top-ten university business school.

Had I acted on my first thought, I never would have known I was specifically hand selected for the new role. Just because I could have cried "racial discrimination" doesn't mean I should have.

If I had taken a racial stance, it would have been reinforced by friends, family, and society. Then, once a lawsuit is filed in a corporate environment, nobody can talk about it anymore. Communication stops because anything said can be used in court. The true story probably never would have come out. I never would have known I had been chosen intentionally for my position and my relationship with the company would have been tarnished. They may have settled with me somehow, but I would have burned a bridge unnecessarily.

These days, people are so quick to call racial discrimination, but what if we all paused to look closer at a situation before jumping to conclusions? I almost misinterpreted my boss's intention, and I'm so glad I paused and waited for an opportunity to talk to him.

What is acceptable in society is not always in our best interest. We need to consider the consequences of our choices. And we need to consider the impact our choices have on those around us. As I discovered, life is so much more rewarding when we live according to biblical mores such as kindness, peacemaking, faithfulness, gentleness, and self-control.

## TRUST IN GOD'S BIGGER PLAN

We all make mistakes. Failures happen, decisions are made, and consequences, whether good or bad, follow our actions.

Our first emotional reactions usually are not our best. But if we don't react immediately, we might discover that God often has a bigger plan.

The book of First Samuel in the Bible tells the story of how David was anointed king of Israel ten years before he received his crown. However, it was not an easy waltz down a red-carpet aisle for David to get to the throne. His life was threatened by King Saul and he spent years in hiding to escape Saul's wrath. David could have killed Saul on a few different occasions, but he chose not to. Just because he could have killed Saul doesn't mean he should have. Instead, he waited for God's timing. He trusted that God had called him to become king, and in due time, God elevated him to that position over Israel.

I have learned to take the lessons from Bible stories like this to heart, and I am committed to living by the principles within them. Over time, God has proven to me that His ways are higher, and His plans are for my good.

Circumstances arise for various reasons. They are not necessarily personal or racial or evil. When life throws a curve ball or we are presented with temptation, it is foolish to run with our emotional reactions. Instead, we are wise to be still, wait, and allow God to work.

# 5: COMFORT VERSUS TRUST

Our first few years of marriage were wonderful. Sheila and I were in love and building a future together. I had landed a good job when I got out of the army, and Sheila was working on her master's degree in communication. Life seemed easy and comfortable. I didn't feel any need to attend church, especially since the churches we had always attended were more like ceremonial social clubs than places of Christ-centered teaching and worship. It was all about dressing up and looking good. They "do church" with nice choir music, but they don't seem to connect with God. After feel-good Sunday services, I saw little fruit in people's lives.

I always felt I lived a better life than the people in those churches. I came to believe church was merely a Sunday community activity because it was socially acceptable. As a young adult, I figured if that is what church is, I didn't need it. It was not relevant for me. I still believed in God, but I thought I had better things to do with my time.

I would soon discover God had so much more for Sheila and me.

My first job after I left the army took me to Dallas, Texas. I moved into an apartment there, and Sheila stayed with her parents in Oklahoma while she was finishing her master's degree. We met on weekends to spend time together, which was a decent temporary arrangement. One weekend that winter, an ice storm hit Texas and Oklahoma. It was a deep freeze that made roads nearly impassable, and it wasn't safe for Sheila to drive down to see me. Just when I thought I'd have to spend that weekend alone, a family friend invited me to church. Funny how God seems to find you when you least expect Him. My first thought was, "Oh, no, not that. No, thank you." But I went to church with her and her family anyway so as not to disappoint a family friend.

The church was Oak Cliff Bible Fellowship, and Tony Evans was the pastor. I noticed right away there was no loud preaching, no holy-roly ceremonial social club, no souped-up choir. Evans was a graduate of Dallas Theological Seminary and the first Black pastor to earn a PhD there. I had never heard the Bible taught how he teaches it. His sermon centered around an understanding of what the Bible meant in a certain time and culture, and then how it was applicable today and relevant for my life.

My goal had been to go to one church service and get out, only to be polite to my friend. But Tony Evans' message that Sunday changed my life. He was teaching from the book of Ephesians regarding the armor of God, and I sensed God speaking to me. I realized Satan knows if he can destroy a marriage. He destroys the kids and the grandchildren for generations. I saw it happen in my own family, and I knew I didn't want it to happen to the family Sheila and I would have.

It was such a transformational experience that I kept going back to that church, and Sheila went with me after a bit of reluctance at first. At Evans' church, they teach their members the principles of the Kingdom of God, so they learn to function under the authority of the Kingdom in every dimension of life. Until my first visit there, I had no idea how important those principles would be in my life, but they would soon become the guidance system that would lead to life-saving events and successes I couldn't have imagined.

I credit my relationship with God to that church. Sheila and I attended services there for a year, and I was baptized there before we moved away. I still have my baptism certificate in a file with our family birth certificates.

At twenty-seven years old, I prayed the sinner's prayer, became "born again," and that laid my spiritual foundation for the rest of my life. I credit that transformation to the success of my marriage. Almost four decades later, I'm the only one of my siblings whose kids have grown up with both their mother and their father at home. As I mentioned before, my siblings took different paths in their lives and had multiple relationships.

Around that same time, the Rodney King riots happened and African Americans did not feel safe in White communities.[5]

---

5   https://www.npr.org/2017/04/26/524744989/when-la-erupted-in-anger-a-look-back-at-the-rodney-king-riots

Tony talked about how we could settle racism if we all simply lived through the Bible. If we just lived as Christians, we could model harmony and acceptance. He read "There is neither Jew nor Gentile, neither slave nor free, nor is there male and female, for you are all one in Christ Jesus" (Galatians 3:28).

The problem was that Christians really didn't model unity in Christ. Pastor Evans said we all need to stop labeling ourselves as a Black Christian or a White Christian. We shouldn't put the Creator of the universe and His Son in a secondary position describing ourselves. He addressed the congregation, "Are you Black first or Christian first? You're a Christian first. That's how you identify." It was easy for everyone there to clap that night because 90 percent of the congregation was Black.

We moved to Tulsa, Oklahoma, after I got a promotion in my job. We tried to find a good Bible teaching church in the Black community there, but we couldn't find one. I didn't want to go to the kind of churches where we used to go, so we searched the yellow pages (because there was no Internet) and found a pastor who had graduated from Dallas Theological Seminary. We were excited to visit his church the next Sunday.

When Sheila and I walked into the sanctuary, I noticed big windows and rows of seats facing the platform. I scanned the crowd of about 500 people and realized we were the only Black people in the whole place. We felt extremely uncomfortable, but we sat down anyway. The people were very gracious to us, greeting us with genuine warmth and hospitality, and the service seemed life-giving. Afterward, however, we thought it might be best to find a church in our Black community due to the racial tension brought on by the Rodney King beating and riots. So, we looked again, and we still couldn't find a Bible teaching church that ministered to our tribe. We didn't want to go back to the old style we had grown up with, so with trepidation we returned to the all-White church.

We were pleasantly surprised when Pastor Bruce Ewing welcomed us and invited us to meet him for lunch. He said he sensed we were leaders and that we could help not only his members, but other Black Christians see their congregation as a welcoming church. He wanted us to know we were wanted at his church and loved unconditionally. After that conversation with him, we decided to attend the church regularly.

All of our friends and family said, "Don't do it. They're going to treat you bad. You know you shouldn't go there." While we respected their concerns, we decided to go there anyway. Because we're Christians first, not Black first.

Some of our friends tried to guilt trip us. "You're leaving your culture behind. You're deserting your heritage."

"I'm not deserting anyone," I said. "I want to go where the Bible is being taught and I don't care what they look like."

Despite their opposition and the odd feeling of being the only Blacks, we attended that church. Those people treated us with love and kindness. I suppose there could have been some people bothered by our presence there, but we never encountered them. It was different, but it felt right. I wasn't looking to be a trailblazer. I just wanted good Bible teaching and I wanted us to grow in our faith. I didn't want to be stagnant. Over time, some of those people became lifelong friends.

We joined a small group and participated there for a year. During that time, Sheila became pregnant with our first child. One evening after our daughter was born, we heard a knock on our door. I opened the door to find some people from the church holding casseroles and salad bowls. When we told our family they had brought us dinner, they couldn't believe it.

"They did *what*? Really? People don't even do that at our church!"

People from church kept bringing meals over for several days afterward. We felt blessed and loved, but our family didn't know what to think of their generosity.

After three years in Tulsa, I received another promotion that took us to South Central Texas. Family members immediately began advising us to find a good Black church again because, "You're going down into the South. Texas was a Confederate state. It won't be the same as that church in Oklahoma." We looked for another good Bible teaching church, but we couldn't find one with a predominantly Black congregation.

Someone suggested we check out Max Lucado at Oak Hills Church of Christ, so we went to visit one Sunday. Max is an outstanding Bible teaching pastor, but at that time, I didn't know anything about the Church of Christ. I was fascinated to learn they sang only acapella, no musical instruments. They offered a six-week new member class in which Lucado said, "Here at this church we major in the majors and we minor in the minors. The Holy Trinity of God is major. But if you're here for the worship, you're not majoring in the majors. You're majoring in the minors." I agreed with that, and I did a lot of lip syncing because, trust me, nobody wants to hear me singing without instruments.

We attended Max Lucado's church for a year, and we appreciated having a choice of three different services. The teaching we received there deepened our faith and our resolve to put God first in every aspect of our lives. But what was especially transformative for us was the aftermath of a serious car accident.

## TRAGEDY AND MIRACLES

During our time in central Texas, I had to attend a weekend conference in Corpus Christi for my job. It was about three to four hours south of San Antonio by car. By then our first son had been born, and it was our tenth anniversary, so I took Sheila and the kids with me. Our daughter, Ashley, was two, and Josh was just a few weeks old. On the way back, we pulled over on the side of the interstate and the next thing I knew I was in a hospital bed and my face was bandaged.

A man driving a cargo van had fallen asleep going seventy miles an hour and rear-ended our car. I have no memory of the accident or of my week-long stay in the hospital, but a state trooper and some witnesses later told us I was out of the car when it happened. I don't know if I was attending to the kids in the backseat or checking a tire, but the impact caused me to flip over the car and into the middle of the highway.

The driver in the car following behind the van that hit us happened to be a pediatric resident in medical school in San Antonio. She stopped immediately and jumped out with a little black bag of medical supplies. She resuscitated our daughter, Ashley, then rushed to check on me.

The left side of my face was crushed and bleeding. She quickly inserted an NG tube down my throat to clear the airway so I could breathe. I was unconscious but alive, so she attended to Sheila and Josh next. Sheila had been knocked unconscious in the driver's seat, the left side of her face bleeding. Josh was safe in his car seat in the backseat even though our car was crushed to half its size. It's a miracle none of us died immediately.

Three helicopters came to airlift Sheila to Wilford Hall Medical Center in San Antonio, Ashley to University Hospital to San Antonio, and me to a hospital in Corpus Christi. Josh was taken by ambulance to a local hospital and later released with little to no injuries. Someone contacted Sheila's sister who took care of him while the rest of us were in the hospital.

I learned later that I was rushed into surgery to repair an orbital blowout fracture (my eye socket had ruptured). The surgeon installed plastic plates and screws on the left side of my face.

Sheila had to have her jaw wired shut for six weeks so the bones in her face could heal. She could only drink protein shakes. Thankfully, she was able to resume nursing Josh after she got home.

Two-year-old Ashley was in a coma for three days. Her recovery from the coma was an absolute miracle. Afterward, she had to relearn to walk and talk in occupational therapy. She has suffered from the effects of a traumatic brain injury (TBI) ever since.

It has been almost twenty-five years and I still have no memory of the accident or of my hospitalization. The only thing I remember is a week or so after I was released from the hospital, my brother told me about the day he and my father came to take me home.

He said there was an older White man sitting in a chair next to my bed. Surprised to see a stranger there, my father asked, "Who are you? What are you doing here?"

The man looked up and said, "My daughter goes to the same church as your son, and we didn't want him to be alone." He said he'd been sitting beside me for three days.

To this day, I've never met him, but my father and brother couldn't deny his kindness.

My father grew up in South Carolina in the '50s when the south was still segregated. Those memories left him with a negative perception of White people. He believed you had to be careful because White people will harm you or do bad things. It shook his paradigm to see a White person showing compassion for his son.

He asked the man, "Why are you here if you don't know him? And you've been sitting here for three days?"

The man answered, "Well, because your son and my daughter go to the same church. And we want to show love through Christ Jesus."

My father and brother were amazed, once again, at the generosity and compassion coming from strangers. A decade later, I learned the man's name was Roland Blair and his daughter Tiffany Jennings was the woman sitting at Ashley's bedside when she awoke.

We had been at Max Lucado's church for a year, but we didn't know many people except for those in our small group. We learned later that several people had signed up for twenty-four-hour rotations at Ashley's bedside. They sang songs and read Bible stories to her around the clock.

Members of our church were parents for our daughter when we couldn't be parents ourselves. Even today, when I think of how they cared for Ashley, tears well up in my eyes. We were told that in the middle of the third night, Ashley began to awake from her coma.

She started blinking, and Tiffany Jennings exclaimed in her big, West Texas accent, "Whoa, my gosh, oh, my gosh! Ashley, are you okay?" Then she ran to let the nurse know Ashley was waking up from her coma.

A week after we all got out of our respective hospitals, we went to see our doctors. Each of our doctors gaped at us in awe when they read the report of what had happened. They stared at me, then at Sheila, then back at me. "This is incredible. You shouldn't even be able to walk, let alone be alive," one of them said.

Even though Ashley had some cognitive challenges due to the TBI, she scored higher on the ACT test than I had. Today she is a graduate of Colorado Christian University, and she has a low-stress job that's perfect for her.

Sheila and I both have some residual pain, but we are so grateful we all lived through the trauma and none of us ended up severely impaired.

The whole ordeal was transformative for me. We all saw a side of humanity and Christian love I didn't know existed. We didn't know any of the people who sat with us in the hospital. We later met Tiffany Jennings, the woman who sat at Ashley's bedside for three days. She and her husband Paul have been dear friends ever since.

We also didn't know the pediatric resident who had stopped at the scene of the accident to help us, but when we found out who she was, we made her a Christmas video and mailed it to her. In it, we all took turns saying thank you and God bless you for saving our lives. Little Ashley was the cutest when she spoke in her little toddler voice, "Thank you for saving my life." We'll never know if all of us would have lived if that woman had not been driving the same highway that day.

People we didn't even know showed up to help us. It is the greatest example of Christians caring for other Christians who are hurt or in need, without qualifications and regardless of what they look like. My family had a chance to see that all White people are not the same. Because most of our siblings are older than Sheila and me, they had memories of violence and hatred between Blacks and Whites from the '70s. It was mind-blowing for them to witness such kindness.

Human beings crave certainty. It's easy to stay in places where we know what to expect from others. We feel safe in familiar surroundings. But growth and transformation happen when we step beyond our self-imposed safety nets. As Sheila and I obeyed God and dared to follow His promptings to venture into unknown communities, God met us there. And not only did

He meet us there, but He revealed Himself to us in ways we never would have seen before. As Henry Blackaby wrote, "God proved to be more than just my Creator or Savior. He was also my sustainer, counselor, comforter, teacher, strength, protector, guide, and much more."[6]

During our recovery season, Sheila and I made a commitment to always trust God to direct our life choices. We didn't know where that commitment would take us, but we chose to lean into Joshua 1:9. "Have I not commanded you? Be strong and courageous. Do not be afraid; do not be discouraged, for the LORD your God will be with you wherever you go." After the accident and those first years in Bible teaching churches, we knew we could take God at His word, regardless of obstacles or opposition.

## COUNTERCULTURAL CHOICES

Of course, any time we make commitments, resistance and obstacles show up. After Ashley was born, Sheila felt led to stay home and be a full-time mom. Though she had her master's degree and had begun a promising career, she believed she needed to be fully present for our daughter and future children. The phone started ringing almost immediately. Friends and relatives were worried.

"What are you doing, Sheila? You're passing up all that money, wasting your education?" they asked. "You're so much better than that," they insisted.

---

6    Blackaby, Henry T. *Experiencing God: Knowing and Doing the Will of God.* B&H Books. May, 2021.

At the time, her decision was countercultural. It was expected that a woman with an education would work to earn a second income for her family. We admire educated career women, and we would never disparage anyone who chooses that path, but Sheila wanted to invest her talents in our children and family.

We noticed that many Christians, regardless of race, seem to be more committed to culture rather than to Christ. We chose to live out our faith according to the Bible, regardless of what friends and relatives said, and no matter how difficult it felt.

Due to my corporate job, we relocated five times when the kids were of school age. As a result, we decided to homeschool for continuity of the education, and we got flack for doing so. Even in the late 1990s, not many people were educating their children at home. Every time we went home for holidays or family gatherings our relatives grilled us with questions.

"Did you put those kids in school yet?"

"Aren't you concerned about their socialization?"

That went on for eleven years. Finally, during year twelve, their opinions shifted. "You guys are so smart, homeschooling those kids. Your children are such great kids compared to students in public schools." The conversation totally flipped. They saw the wisdom of our decision, even though it took them more than a decade to respect it.

If we had listened to our extended family's fears, we never would have known what could be. All five of our kids are grown up and doing great. No one has three eyes.

As a result of homeschooling, our children developed a strong bond with each other and they are still close to one another. It's almost like the Waltons. We have a family group text and everyone says goodnight to each other every evening. The kids also have their own group text thread. Even though they don't all live under the same roof anymore, they stay in touch like best friends.

Some people think it's weird for siblings to be so close, but I think it's sad that families scatter and don't stay connected. We need each other now more than ever in this world. I've had a vision prayer for a long time, even before the accident, that we would someday have a large property where we can live close to each other. Life is easier when you're surrounded with people who love and support you. It's hard when you're isolated.

As countercultural as it was (and still is), Sheila and I chose to live out our faith according to the Bible. Galatians 1:10 says, "Am I now trying to win the approval of human beings, or of God? Or am I trying to please people? If I were still trying to please people, I would not be a servant of Christ." Our friends and relatives tried to give us well-intentioned advice, but we knew we couldn't make decisions to make them happy. It wasn't always fun, but it was worth it.

At a certain point, you get used to swimming against the current. You become a strong swimmer. God's instruction in the Bible is not meant to be restrictive. Rather, He's trying to protect us from the calamities that can happen based on the choices we make in life. He has given us a prescription for success, a guidance system that, when followed, sets us up for fulfillment in every area of our lives.

Cultural norms cause people to believe it's acceptable to drink excessively, do drugs, and have multiple sexual partners. But I've never met anyone who would say, "I wish I'd done more drugs" or "I should have had more lovers." On the other hand, I have heard plenty of people, myself included, say things like, "After thirty-five years, my marriage is more rewarding and loving than it was at the beginning."

We must be willing to go through the valleys to experience the mountain tops. When we walk together with God and follow His instructions, the valleys don't seem as steep because we grow through those tough times.

Sheila and I invested a lot of money and time into our marriage by participating in Christian counseling. Secular counselors say divorce is an option. But that means you can be divorced many times, and life can become painfully complex.

Sometimes people assume I'm successful due to military experience and lessons learned in my childhood, but they tend to overlook my faith. I'm not perfect or special, but I have a compass that guides me in the right direction. Without that compass I would be drifting with the culture and maintaining the status quo with no guidance system at all.

In Henry Blackaby's workbook, *Experiencing God*, he included a seven-step diagram. In step one, God desires to have us work with Him to build His kingdom. In step two, God pursues relationship with us. Step three, He invites us to join Him.

Step four includes God speaking to us. In step five, we experience a crisis of belief.

Step six is where we either adjust our life to follow God or get stuck in the status quo. That's where most people stop because sometimes God calls us into situations that don't make logical sense. We hesitate when our friends and relatives say we're crazy. We hold ourselves back because we're uncertain of the outcome.

Step seven in Blackaby's diagram is where we obey God's call and experience the spiritual growth and adventure He intends for us.

At one point in my career, I was offered a position that would pay $270,000 per year. I gave it serious consideration because I wanted the health care and to be able to pay my bills. I wanted the job title and the certainty it would give me. At the same time, I had an opportunity to join a start-up company that designed products to help cancer patients.

As I prayerfully weighed both options, I asked myself, "Am I going to take hold of the comfort of certainty, or am I going to trust God and step out in a new direction?

I could have stalled out on step six and taken the path of least resistance. The high-paying job would have been easy to accept. But I am convinced God was moving me to do the hard thing rather than the expected thing. I joined the start-up and never looked back.

I believe God wants us to take actions that don't make logical sense so we can point to it and say, "God did this, not me" when we experience success.

Sheila and I chose to be obedient even when it didn't make sense. We have been blessed in our lives because we trusted God. When Sheila said she wanted to stay home with our children, we adjusted our lives so we could afford to live on one salary. Within a few years, I was earning my income plus what Sheila previously made, and we never felt deprived. God provided for us like the prophet's oil that never ran out.

We didn't tell very many people what we were doing because they would have thought we were crazy. We quietly obeyed God, and my decision to join the start-up company proved to be the best choice. We launched a great product into the marketplace as a pilot. And because that product was a pilot, I couldn't do anything more until it ran its course. With that opening in my calendar, I was able to take a leave of absence to run for Congress in 2020. I would not have been able to do that if I was working a corporate job.

The corporate job would have had me traveling away from home 70 percent of the time. Sheila felt that would be hard on our growing family and that option didn't sit well with her. I trust my wife. We trust each other, because in marriage, it's not two people but one. Listening to Sheila, I realized that job wasn't the right choice. I'll do anything to provide for my family, but I prayed about it and trusted that the start-up was the right move. It didn't pay as much, but I knew I could trust God to make up the difference.

We can't know all God's plans and purposes, and sometimes He leads us into uncertain waters, but we can trust He is with us always, even when we make impulsive choices out of pride, fear, or uncertainty, as I have done in the past.

# 6: Simple but Not Easy

I n America, it's common to believe the path to a fulfilled life is to go to college, start a lifelong career, get married, have children, retire, and play golf. At least that's how we've been told life should go. It sounds simple, but it's not that easy. In reality, we may or may not go to college, we might change careers several times, and if we get married, many of us end up divorced, which means our children are raised in single parent households like I was. Finance is not taught in school, so most of us are ill equipped to even consider retirement, and we're too busy trying to survive to learn how to play golf.

Having lived my early years with my mother in poverty and then with my military father who was rarely interested in my life, I didn't have much help with academics or planning for higher education. I didn't come from a college educated family. Some of my relatives didn't even finish high school.

Prep schools make entering and succeeding in college easier, but I went to a general education high school because that was what was available to me back then. My parents didn't know how to help me prepare for college or how to pay for it.

School was challenging for me largely because I have dyslexia, which means I have difficulty with reading and writing. I struggled to get good grades. There were classes I could have taken if I was on a college track, but my parents and counselors didn't steer me toward them. It seemed nobody expected me to be college material, so they didn't initiate the kind of conversations with me that they had with other students.

I only took the ACT test once, not knowing I could take it multiple times and use the best score for college applications. Lacking my parents' financial help, I paid for my own education by working full time while serving in the army reserves and attending a full load of classes.

It's common to be critical of our parents, but it's better to forgive them for what they never had. Parents can't teach their children what they didn't learn themselves. Parents can't give their children something they don't have or never experienced. My parents knew education was important, but they didn't know the steps to get there. Early on, they didn't teach me the importance of reading or developing good study habits. However, I ultimately learned to appreciate how they instilled a strong work ethic, honesty, and tenacity in me.

I like to say I graduated "Magna Cum Lucky" from college, but truthfully, I worked hard through college and every post graduate degree program afterward because I was determined never to live in poverty again. The struggle nearly got the best of me at one point and I came close to quitting college in my junior year. I was ready to give up, but Sheila and her sister convinced me to stay. After that, I pushed myself harder and I was able to achieve the education I wanted. I figured I could have excuses or I could decide to get it done. I am grateful I hung in there even when it seemed like an impossible mountain to climb.

Through it all, I came to understand that outstanding leaders live on a growth continuum, a path of continuous improvement, which caused me to desire knowledge that would expand my understanding of life, meaning, and purpose. I became a lifelong learner. I learned to love learning, studying, and discovering new knowledge. I have frequented some major college campuses every couple of years for continuing education throughout my adult life, including the Wharton School in Philadelphia, Columbia University, and the University of Chicago. I feel so young every time I step onto a college campus.

With all my formal education, I accumulated stature, which means I could boast about what I know, but I've found that biblical training is instruction in humanity and wholehearted living. When it comes to navigating relationships, finances, and major life decisions, the Bible provides the wisdom I need. Most people simply get an education, then build a career, then chase the American dream, but none of that prepares anyone for marriage.

## Getting Married Is Simple; Staying Married is Not Easy

Sheila and I thought we knew each other well before we got married, even though we hadn't lived together before the wedding like many couples do these days. However, we had spent so much time with her family through high school and beyond that we naturally assumed married life would be easy. We soon found out that getting married is simple but learning to be married is not always easy. In fact, it's hard sometimes.

I had already been living in the apartment before our wedding. It was a small, one-bedroom abode that I kept organized and neat due to my military upbringing and subsequent service. In anticipation of Sheila moving in and beginning our life as newlyweds, I rearranged my personal belongings to make space for hers. The bathroom was small and had only one sink, so I carefully moved my shaving cream, razor, and aftershave to one side of the only cabinet. Sheila then proceeded to load the cabinet up with all kinds of girly stuff. Strike number one.

Due to the lack of space, we agreed to share one tube of toothpaste. It wasn't long before I noticed that Sheila squeezed the toothpaste tube in the middle. I always squeezed the toothpaste from the end and smoothed it out, as it "should be" handled. Day after day, I would get up in the morning and see that she had mutilated the toothpaste tube yet again. Strike number two.

I know, it sounds cliché and petty, but it was a big deal to me at the time. *Who does this?* I wondered. I was flabbergasted that the woman I married was not the girl I thought I knew. I had to say something to alleviate my angst.

"Honey, could you just squeeze the toothpaste from the end and smooth it out instead of squishing it in the middle?" I asked.

"What's wrong with how I squeeze the toothpaste?" she responded.

"It's messy. This is going to be a problem," I said.

I had never seen this side of her even after dating for seven years. *What else do I not know about her? Does she kick puppies?* I wondered. I didn't think I could get used to it.

She refused to change her toothpaste mutilating ways, and I had to learn to live with the atrocious sight until Proctor and Gamble came out with a toothpaste pump. It saved our marriage.

I'm a neat freak and Sheila is not. As we adjusted to life under the same roof, I learned that some things call for compromise or change and some require letting go. At first it seemed like a no-compromise issue, but the toothpaste ordeal didn't rise to the level of a serious problem. It was simply an indicator of our quirky personalities that we had to get used to. In marriage, you have to pick your battles.

Our first argument might seem benign, but it felt like a big deal to me. We've been married for more than three decades now, and the toothpaste saga lives on. We now have separate sink vanities. Her side is a mess, and her toothpaste tube always looks like it lost a fight with Mike Tyson. We laugh about how serious it seemed all those years ago.

After we moved beyond that fiasco, I figured it was time to plan for our future. So, I brought it up one evening at dinner.

"When we have kids, I'd like for you to stay home with them," I said. I assumed she'd be happy to have my support for that.

"No. I have my career and I plan to work," she replied. "Why are we even talking about this when we don't have kids yet?"

"We should have that settled before we have children," I said. She did not agree. It was clear we were not in agreement on that issue. The look on her face told me there was nothing I could say or do to convince her.

Sheila and I are both strong willed, so naturally we valued our own opinions. We called ourselves Christians, but we weren't anchored together in faith until I was baptized about five years into our marriage. Up until then, we didn't see eye to eye on various issues. We had disagreements because we weren't aligned with a specific guidance system. Sheila had her upbringing and family, I had mine, and neither of them gave us consistently good advice. We loved each other, but nothing unified us on a sense of compromise or care for one another's heart.

Sheila was close to her seven siblings. She called her four sisters every day and it was as if she had one foot in her family and one foot in our marriage. I wasn't exactly close to my own siblings, but that didn't stop them from interjecting their advice on occasion. With so many inconsistent opinions floating around us, we were like a leaky boat on rough sea waters being tossed about and going nowhere.

Once Shelia and I started walking with God together, we discovered a guidance system we could share. We became less and less affiliated with and influenced by our respective families. Ultimately, we became our own family with God at the center.

The big turning point in our marriage was when we took the new believers' class at Tony Evans' church. I learned that if I became the spiritual leader in my family, I would experience more harmony with my wife. There would be light, truth, and comfort for my wife. I wouldn't be perfect but I could create trust there if I took the lead in following Christ.

Given that more women attend church and Bible studies than men, this is an uncommon path for husbands to take. But the rewards are greater than I even imagined they would be.

Almost every newlywed has the thought that they married the wrong person. Sheila and I each had our doubts in our early years, but joining together in one faith solidified our marriage. As the years have passed I've become more and more certain I married the right woman. I am proud to call her my wife, the love of my life, and the mother of my children.

## HAVING KIDS IS FUN; RAISING THEM IS NOT EASY

After our first child, Ashley, was born, Sheila changed her mind about her career and decided to stay home to raise our family. She sacrificed her master's degree and career. As I mentioned earlier, when her friends and family members heard about her choice, the phone rang incessantly for several days with people saying, "What are you thinking? You're better than this. You're going to waste your education and lose all the money you could be making."

I never thought about how much money she could have made. I've never quantified lost income. Even as we were bombarded with people's opinions, we knew the time and attention we poured into our children would be worth the sacrifice. In the years to come, we found it was not a sacrifice at all. It was an investment that reaped unimaginable rewards and joy.

In the early years, we learned that babies are precious but sleepless nights are exhausting, and toddlers are cute but disciplining them is not fun. I was so happy and proud to be a dad, and I still am. However, we didn't know what we didn't know, so we took parenting classes and I read Dr. Dobson's book *Dare to Discipline*.

Our first test came with Josh, our second born. Josh was barely two years old and still in diapers at the time. We had instructed him to keep his food and sippy cup drinks in the kitchen. We wanted to teach him to stay out of the family room with his snacks to avoid the inevitable sticky messes toddlers can make.

One evening, he stepped one cute little toddler foot on the edge of the carpet in the family room just to test us. He stood there grinning at us with a sippy cup in one hand and a cookie in the other.

"Josh, what did we tell you?" I said.

He didn't move. He stood there in total defiance, daring me with his eyes to enforce our instructions. Knowing "whoever spares the rod hates their children, but the one who loves their children is careful to discipline them" (Prov. 13:24), I gave Josh a swift but loving spanking. Yes, toddlers are cute, but disciplining them is not fun.

Everyone, including grandparents, siblings, neighbors, and friends, had parenting advice for us. Their opinions were as conflicting and inconsistent as their marriage advice had been a few years earlier. But we wanted to raise our kids with Biblical principles. Kids don't obey or say please and thank you on their own. They need training, so Sheila and I based our training from a biblical perspective.

We believed in discipline and boundaries. We didn't want to be friends with our kids. We were their mother and father, not their buddies. We made some hard decisions along the way. We replaced the television with books and outdoor activities. Because I traveled so much during the week, I chose to be home with the family on weekends rather than head to the golf course to network with work colleagues. I refused weekend junkets with the guys at the office. It felt like a sacrifice at times, but it was so worth it.

We also chose to homeschool our kids back when people in the corporate world didn't do that. Sheila did most of the planning and teaching and I trusted her completely. Our goal was to have them become educated, mature, and responsible adults, and they did. Regardless of what education they choose or what career paths they take, we are proud to have raised upstanding citizens.

That sounds so simple, yet it wasn't easy. Before they all grew up, we had to navigate the teen phase. We relocated because of my job five times during their childhood years. The moves had an impact on their friendships. We had to have some come to Jesus conversations with our oldest and youngest sons on different occasions.

Thankfully, none of the kids did drugs or smoked cigarettes, but one of our sons had an attraction to a girl in the homeschool co-op when they were both thirteen years old. Another corporate relocation required that we move away, and he could no longer see her. We soon noticed a dramatic change in his behavior. Teenagers deal with a lot of hormonal changes as they mature.

They seem to be either happy or mad, and they don't know how to identify or convey their emotions. My son was angry, and his behavior around the house was disruptive. He became a bully and picked on his siblings. It seemed like every time we turned around, the boys were fighting and the girls were crying. If there was drama in the house, he was involved.

In one of our parenting classes, Sheila and I learned we were dealing with a $500 reaction to a fifty-cent issue. We had to enforce discipline in our home as well as teach our son to trust God to help him through his emotions.

One summer, that same son went to a camp that was led by a guy who was a retired missionary. He came back with a much better attitude toward life and our family. Later he raised his own funds for a mission trip to Central America. He completed a four-year college degree and got married right after graduation. Sheila and I thank God we were unified on how we should raise our children and the biblical standard we adhered to. We were not perfect parents by any means, however, we felt we were guided by compass of truth.

## FAMILY LIFE LOOKS SIMPLE, BUT IT'S NOT EASY

I had a wonderful career for many years and I also had challenges along the way. Having a family may sound simple, but it's not easy, especially if you have a generational vision for your family. At times it can feel like a tremendous burden for a husband and father.

At one point as I was going through some job changes, Sheila and I found ourselves neck-deep in spiritual warfare. For seven months we would get into an argument, then reconcile. The pattern became nerve-racking, and I wondered, *Has the clock run out on our marriage? Is this what it looks like when a marriage ends?*

Instead of running with those thoughts, we agreed to participate in Henry Blackaby's Bible study, *Experiencing God.* As we worked through the twelve lessons of biblical teaching in that program, Sheila and I came to know God intimately, to recognize His voice, and to understand His will for our lives. That training reawakened my passion for my faith and helped heal our marriage.

We were also mentored by some great pastors over the course of our journey such as Joe Stowell, former president of Moody Bible Institute and executive pastor of a church we attended in Chicago. Additionally, we attended several Family Life "Weekend to Remember" conferences hosted by Dennis and Barbara Rainey. Through them, we learned what it means to be husband and wife and what is God's design for marriage. Like taking our car in for a tune up, we always felt like we revved up our relationship out of those conferences.

Biblical training gave us wisdom we never would have found elsewhere. I came to realize I can get knowledge in traditional education, but I can't get wisdom or humility on that track. The uncommon path I've taken includes the spiritual aspect of life. The more I learn, the more I realize what I didn't know. I believe in being a lifelong learner, not to hoard knowledge, but to gain wisdom, which the Bible says is more precious than gold.

I once told a friend I planned to work my corporate gig, retire, then move to Arizona and pick up golf. "When you do that, Satan will leave you alone," he said. "You're basically checking out of life. From a scriptural standpoint, God has been preparing you for something all these years, and you're basically taking off the jersey and quitting. People think they'll volunteer here or there when they retire, but they rarely do. The battle line is in our schools and communities. Checking out will cause you to miss out." I knew he was right, and I'm glad I listened to his wisdom.

Christians often ask God to bless their plans. But God is inviting us to follow Him. It's as if He says, "Follow me; my plans are already blessed." I've found that to be so true. Training and ongoing biblical education has made me more aware of where God wants me to go. That's why I ran for Congress, ran for Governor of Minnesota, and founded our nonprofit organization, TakeCharge. Sheila and I were recently invited to speak at a local church on the topic of restoring Christ in the Black family. We are passionate about this message and we're certain that is where God is leading us.

Putting God in the center of my marriage, raising kids in faith apart from cultural norms, and persevering on my educational track were all uncommon choices. My family, friends, and acquittances thought, and still believe, we were odd people. They said I was going off the deep end, selling out the Black community and trying to be someone I'm not. Many of us were never encouraged to excel in school or seek higher education. We were rarely advised to invest in spiritual growth or work on our marriage and parenting relationships. Sadly, many marriages end in divorce, especially among Black couples, leaving moms to raise the kids alone. But it doesn't have to be that way. Taking charge of my own life by submitting to God has made all the difference in the world. That may seem like a radical idea, but it is how the vast majority of Americans lived for decades. It was only recent history that made the teachings of Christ and biblical standards of life passé.

Doing the right thing and living a godly life seems simple, but circumstances are not always easy. Taking the simple and easy route makes people play small and keeps us from living a God-sized life. God never promised anyone an easy life, but His ways are surprisingly simple and rewarding to follow when we choose to.

# 7: A Culture in Crisis

I was six years old, and my younger brother was four when our parents divorced. As young boys, we watched our older siblings make choices that took them deep into poverty and depravity. We came from the same parents, lived in the same places, and were exposed to the same cultural nuances. I walked away thinking I would never want to go through that again, and I wouldn't want my children to experience that lifestyle either. However, even after living in Hawaii and Oklahoma with our father for several years, my brother must have interpreted it all differently than I did.

My brother got married in his twenties. He was an assistant manager at Domino's Pizza, and he and his new wife lived in an apartment. Unfortunately, his wife wanted a more affluent life-style than they could afford, and they got into financial trouble with debt. They ended up divorced and he left, disconnecting from his young daughter. He moved to New York where the only people he knew were our mom and our older siblings. He soon got caught up in the local culture, using and dealing drugs. He got arrested, which broke our mom's heart. Her youngest child, her baby, was in prison.

I called my brother after he was released from jail. "You have a car," I said. "Fill the gas tank and drive as far south as you can. You might get as far as North Carolina. Make your mark there." I hoped he would choose to better his life by going someplace new and adapting to a healthier culture. He would get excited about new decisions, but you never knew what he was really thinking. His decisions were often disconnected from rational thought.

For whatever reason, he didn't want to take my advice. He stayed in his New York comfort zone, most likely out of familiarity. I think he needed to heal the scar in his heart, and he needed to fill that God-sized hole, the void we all have until we open up to Christ.

My brother and I had the same advantages growing up. He lived in Hawaii and Oklahoma with me and our dad. He went back to the projects in New York while I was serving in the army and beginning my career.

Sadly, my younger brother began shooting up heroine and died at age forty of HIV from contaminated drug needles. He was caught up in a culture he wasn't equipped to withstand.

While I was submitting my life to God, he was being tossed about by every worldly wind. I had talked to him about my faith on several occasions. I didn't hammer my beliefs into him, but he never showed any interest in God or Christ. The toughest part for me when I share my faith with someone in another state is it's hard to help them find a good Bible teaching church in America, especially in the Black community. I didn't know what to recommend.

## OLD PARADIGMS DIE HARD

Most Americans do not interact socially with people outside their own ethnic group. This has more to do with where we grow up geographically and what schools we attend.

When Sheila and I first moved to Tulsa, Oklahoma, we had looked for a church in the Black community. We couldn't find a good bible teaching church, so we joined an all-White church. Our Black friends and family thought we were taking too big a risk. It wasn't considered safe or acceptable for Black people to attend a church outside their own community. We got used to being two of the few Black people in attendance, and sometimes the only Black people there.

It wasn't like we thought White churches were good or Black churches were bad. We just wanted to be involved in a church that taught solid biblical principles to help us grow in our faith. I wasn't willing to compromise.

People would sometimes ask, "Kendall, doesn't it bother you to be around all those White people?"

I would respond with, "What White people? I only see fellow Christians."

I never felt like I had to work hard to fit in, nor was I confused by the color of my skin or the history of our people. In fact, I feel a greater obligation to live a life worthy of their sacrifices.

I identify with Christ, so I'm comfortable in my own space. I don't have to pretend I'm anybody special. I never feel inferior or out of place. I also have no delusions. When I look in the mirror, I see what color my skin is. But I'm a child of God, and I know He loves me. It took me some time to get there, and I had to take that initial step to put myself in situations where I'm the only Black guy in the room. The second and third steps became easier. Now I don't think twice about what color the people around me are. We're all human beings created in God's image.

When we were in our mid-twenties, Sheila and I hosted a small group Bible study in a condo we bought early in our marriage.

One woman who came for the first time looked around our home and said, "Wow, this is not what I expected. This is pretty normal." She had never been in the home of a Black family.

Most people expect Black people to live at or below their standard of living. They've never been a guest in a Black person's home or done a potluck with people of color. Our church friends didn't expect to see such a nice home. Our neighbors were all White, and there weren't many Black families living in middle to upper class neighborhoods in the '80s, '90s, and early 2000s. It's not that we were special, there just weren't many of us. In northern and western areas of the United States, the Black population is sparse. There's nothing wrong with that, it's simple geography that has limited the exposure to Black people.

At church, we didn't dress fancy or wear flashy jewelry. Our outward appearance didn't indicate that we had more income than most families. As my career progressed, we moved into bigger houses in more affluent neighborhoods mainly because we had such a big family with five kids. Looking back now, I can see our presence in those spaces helped to break some barriers. A few of our friends had never stepped foot in a Black family's home. Visiting our home was an experience that seemed radically normal because our home environment was quite similar to their own.

Today it is not unusual to see White and Black Christians worshiping side by side and serving side by side. Sixty years ago, however, if anyone said a Black man and his wife would one day enter a White church in the Deep South and feel welcome, nobody would have believed it. They would say that would never happen, and if it did, the White people would run them out. Our country was still segregated at that time, heading into the post-civil rights movement. Old paradigms die hard, but we've made tremendous progress in this country over the past sixty years.

When our son recently started attending a good Bible teaching church in Franklin, Tennessee, Sheila and I went to visit and received a warm welcome from the congregation. Americans for the most part have opened their hearts and homes to people of all ethnicities. Biracial families are more common than ever across the country. But since 2010, America has been taking steps backward. There seems to be a social and political movement that insists Black people are still oppressed.

Today, Black people are not oppressed in the United States, and it hasn't been that way for decades. We have many disparities, however, most of those disparities are not due to racial bias but driven by the fatherless home crisis. In our lifetime, we have witnessed the Black community radically transform from 80 percent two-parent nuclear families to 80 percent fatherless homes. We are a culture in crisis.

## DIVISION ON THE RISE

Where I live in the Twin Cities in Minnesota, I speak often about two-parent Black families. I recently hosted a seminar featuring Brandon Tatum, a former police officer, who spoke on "Law Enforcement in the Black Community: What the Media Doesn't Reveal." More than 300 people attended the fundraiser, including a local Black pastor. Afterward the pastor posted on social media, "Kendall Qualls should have consulted Black pastors before hosting this event and inviting a grifter like Brandon Tatum." Typically, events like that are vetted and hosted by local Black pastors.

I spoke with another Black pastor in the Twin Cities after reading his social media criticism of me and my statements.

"You're an associate pastor," I said, "When did slandering a fellow Christian in public become the biblical standard of behavior? According to Matthew 18, if you have an issue with a brother in Christ, you go to them directly."

We met at his church and had a bantering discussion on the issues of the Black community.

As we talked further, he said, "You're right, I shouldn't have berated you in social media. I'm sorry."

"We need to fix our culture," I said.

"I agree," he said, "but you don't need to do this in front of White people."

"Look, this has been going on for fifty years. We need to stop being embarrassed about airing our dirty laundry. We need to get this fixed. The quiet acceptance of this behavior in our communities and the destruction of families in our communities is one of the reasons I didn't have any interest in attending church or becoming a Christian as a young adult. Our communities are filled with pastors like Jeremiah Wright doing his performing acts in front the masses and never confronting the underlying problem that is destroying our communities."

"What are you talking about? I love that guy!" he said. "And Louis Farrakhan . . . how else is a Black man supposed to get his identity?"

I answered, "In the Bible. In Galatians. We're neither slave nor free, neither Greek nor Jew, male nor female. We're all one under the cross."

There are many churches that espouse Jeremiah Wright's teachings in every Black community across the country. One of the main reasons I didn't become a Christian at a younger age was I didn't buy into their Black liberation theology. For them, racial identity trumps the cross. They are "Black first, not Christian first."

Black liberation theology originated on July 31, 1966, when fifty-one Black pastors bought a full-page ad in the *New York Times* and demanded a more aggressive approach to eradicating racism. They echoed the demands of the Black power movement, but the new crusade found its source of inspiration in the Bible.[7] Sadly, only 17 percent of Black pastors have a seminary

---

7    https://www.history.com/this-day-in-history/united-states-invades-grenada

degree. Because many of them have limited Bible knowledge, they can't teach what they don't have.

Dwight Hopkins, a professor at the University of Chicago Divinity School, says Black liberation theology often portrays Jesus as a brown-skinned revolutionary. He cites the words of Mary in the Magnificat, also known as the "Song of Mary," in which she says God intends to bring down the mighty and raise the lowly.

The main focus of the Jeremiah Wright churches seems to be on how oppressed Black people are. Eighty to 90 percent of Black churches espouse this philosophy, and it didn't resonate with me. It wasn't until I was invited to Tony Evans' church in Dallas that I understood what Christianity was all about. During our frequent relocations we sought pastors who held to the same framework of biblical teaching, regardless of their skin color.

My motivation is based on truth and the tragedy of the lies and manipulation people are told about racism, disparities, and social justice. It is all a sick agenda of control while so many Black children are growing up without a father in their home, and the streets are overrun with rioting and looting. I call it a culture in crisis. I think their priorities are mixed up. I want to bring positive change to the Black community, and they're worried that I don't consult with them first. They see me as acting outside the Black community. They are like Pharisees seeking only to look good in public.

There was a time in the not too distant past when Black Americans were on the rise. Our challenges were mighty and the institutional barriers to our success were numerous. Yet we clung to a common identity, bound together by pride and a burning passion to overcome. Our faith, traditions, and familial bonds guided us through the darkness toward a better life. Then everything changed. In the 1960s, nearly 80 percent of Black households were two-parent families. Tragically, that was the high watermark.

Over the ensuing decades, marriage rates among Black Americans collapsed while unmarried births exploded. Most of those fatherless children grew up as angry boys and vulnerable girls. The scale of this tragedy is nearly incomprehensive. The values and culture that bound our community were torn down and replaced with a vicious cycle of violence, poverty, and government dependency. All of this took place while public schools crumbled and academic achievement plunged.

The voices that stepped into this void did not provide an aspirational message but rather one of self-serving cynical politics, an elite few seeking to profit from this desperate situation. Rather than offering solutions, they perpetuated the cycle of poverty and violence, stoked racial strife, and fueled more dependency. We are a culture in crisis. Our community is in desperate need of a new voice.

Black communities are crumbling and nobody is addressing it or offering viable solutions. Black Americans are more likely to enter a church to attend a funeral than they are to celebrate a wedding. We are a community in chaos with fatherless homes, near non-existent marriage rates, and spiraling Black-on-Black crime challenging us to the core. I stand for the restoration of two-parent families and what I call "traditional Christian faith" that includes hard work and responsibility.

Sheila and I often feel like a minority in what we teach and stand for, but we're just being obedient to what we believe God has laid on our hearts. It's sad because these are traditional values that used to be taught. Grandma and grandpa would teach the younger generations the principles they probably learned from scripture and from their parents and grandparents.

These days, it's as if a tidal wave of evil has swept across America causing division everywhere. We're divided racially, politically, and morally. We're even divided medically and sexually. People are blaming other people for their problems, and everyone is afraid to stand up. I want to inspire my fellow Americans to take a stand for what is right.

## ONE UNDER THE CROSS

There are two organizations in America that don't get hung up on race: athletics and the military. Athletes in team sports aren't concerned about their teammates' ethnicity. They just want team players who will help them win the game. There are good players and there are players who fumble the ball, but their value as a player has nothing to do with their race. The military is the same. They care more about who has their back than what color the skin on their back is. They're all working for something bigger than themselves. These two groups are less critical of ethnic groups than most other Americans. They judge people by their character and abilities.

Ronald Reagan was president when I was in high school. In 1983, he ordered U.S. forces to invade the island of Grenada due to a threat posed to American nationals on that Caribbean nation, including a group of American medical students. Reagan sent the Marines there to secure the safety of U.S. citizens and pull the American students out. There hadn't been any armed conflict since the Vietnam war up to that time. In little more than a week, Grenada's government was overthrown.[8]

When the Marines arrived, they found where the students were holed up, they busted open the door, and called out, "We're the United States Marines! We're here to rescue the Americans."

"I'm American! I'm American!" the students shouted back, waving their hands and stepping forward. None of them said "I'm African American, I'm Asian American, I'm Native American." Race and color didn't matter in that situation. In my mind, if it's good enough to be American without an ethnicity identifier when someone is saving your life, it's good enough to be a plain old American when you are in school, around the dinner table, in church, in public, or in the marketplace on U.S. shores.

It grieves me that our nation has become so divided over race and so-called social justice issues. Most people don't know they're being manipulated for political reasons. When people come to the United States from other countries and get their citizenship, the first thing they tell their friends and family or post on social media is, "I'm an American now!" To an immigrant, it's an honor to become a citizen here. But so many of us have no idea how valuable and significant it is to be an American citizen. We've lost our gratitude and forgotten why our country

---

8   https://www.history.com/this-day-in-history/united-states-invades-grenada

is so exceptional in the world we live in. Our public schools no longer teach the significant difference between America and other countries.

I was in Detroit in 2008 through 2009, during the height of the recession when Obama was president. The auto industry was hit hard, causing Michigan to become one of the highest union participation states in the country. The unemployment rate hit 15 percent at the time. I was at a Tigers baseball game with about 150 of my team members from work. During the seventh inning stretch as the "Take Me Out to the Ballgame" song blared over the sound system, an announcer broke in and said, "Ladies and gentlemen, we have some people here who have just been sworn in as new United States citizens."

I watched as a small group of people walked out onto the field. I noticed that none of them were White. Some were women from India wearing *saris*, some were African, and others were Asian. All of them waved little American flags as they smiled at the crowds in the stands. The stadium was packed with 90 percent White people, many of them unemployed due to the recession. I wondered if the crowd would boo them for moving into their city and potentially vying for their jobs. But suddenly, as if on cue, the entire crowd stood and started clapping for the new citizens. I thought, *Wow, I didn't see that coming.* I didn't expect the crowd to accept them so wholeheartedly, especially given the way legacy news media portrays America. They gave these new citizens, none of whom looked like them, a standing ovation. Sadly, that event was never featured on the nightly news or posted on social media.

As I write this book, people are crossing our southern borders by the tens of thousands on a weekly basis and they're given special privileges and social welfare benefits. I think that is an insult to the people who came here legally and worked hard to secure their citizenship. It usually takes seven to ten years for some immigrants to complete the process, during which they renounce all claims to any social welfare benefits. It takes tremendous courage for someone to come to America and take all the proper steps to become a citizen here. They do it because they believe they can become anything they want to be in this country.

Friends, there is no need to define ourselves by a one-dimensional framework like ethnicity. We are much more than that. Let's be bold and courageous and stop listening to divisive messages from others. We are all beloved children of God. Let's ditch the status quo and bring healing, truth, and courage back to our culture.

# 8: Removing Negaholics

Throughout my life, well-meaning people have offered advice.

"Don't do that."

"Don't go there."

"You can't trust White people"

"Don't get out of the Army. You're safer there."

"White people will discriminate against you."

I realized they wanted to protect me, but at the same time, I didn't want to live my life in fear. Heeding fear-based negative advice would keep me from success in the bigger world. Regardless of ethnicity, we all have negative voices in our heads and in our communities.

When Sheila and I chose to homeschool our kids, we also chose not to listen to people who insisted we were making a mistake. We had to ignore the advice of family and friends and remain confident in our decision but also be respectful and loving.

Fearful people tend to project their fears onto others, which is what happened when people told us we were making big mistakes in our choices of church and our children's education. They were afraid for us because they wouldn't have felt safe making those kinds of choices for themselves. In their minds, they wouldn't be safe attending a church that was populated predominately by White people, and in some cases, all White people. Some of them thought we put ourselves in danger. And in their thinking, homeschool would be detrimental to their own kids, so surely our children were in jeopardy. They meant well, but Sheila and I were committed to our faith, and it wasn't just a Sunday social club for us.

Before we even had kids of our own, we met a homeschool family at church. They stood out to me because their children were so polite and peaceful while other kids six-years-old and younger were running around shouting, screaming, and bumping into adults that were standing in conversation with other people. While the parents of that family talked to other adults, their children stood quietly alongside them.

I was so impressed with them that I walked over to the father and asked, "Hey, what's the magic here? Why are your kids so calm and mature?" He explained that they chose to homeschool their children and that their behavior reflected what they were taught.

That was our first exposure to home education. I was only twenty-eight-years-old, and we had zero kids at the time. I told Sheila, "We have to look into this." It was like a Sesame Street line: "One of these things is not like the other."

We decided to homeschool our children for several reasons. My corporate relocations were one of the main factors, while other drivers included wanting our kids to be academically successful and have exceptional character.

We soon started looking into the concept and logistics of homeschooling. When our kids were very young, Sheila started teaching them well before they reached school age. As things progressed, we found people who could teach the subjects we didn't feel equipped to teach. We found computer programmers who taught math and retired nurses who taught biology. We learned that teaching our own kids isn't as hard as people think and our that children didn't lack in socialization, which is a common fear among people who are steeped in the public school system.

Some of our friends and family thought our children would not transition well as adults or we would hinder them academically. In their eyes, our kids were not "normal."

## FEARFUL BY NATURE

Humans are fearful by nature. We are wired to avoid danger, which makes it easy for us to assume the worst. Once, when Sheila and I were walking in our neighborhood past a large, wooded area, we heard a sound like leaves and sticks crackling. We wondered if a bear was going to emerge. At the time, we lived in northern New Jersey where black bears are common. We froze in fear for a minute before a little squirrel appeared, twitching his bushy tail. He was probably more afraid than we were. It's funny how quickly the mind perceives the worst.

If there had actually been a bear in those woods, fear would have empowered us to run. The New International Version of the Bible mentions fear or do not be afraid 365 times. That is one "fear not" per day for a whole year. Unfortunately, fear can derail us in subtle ways, especially when we allow the fears of others to influence us.

Sheila and I bought our first house when we were twenty-two years old. Eight months later we bought another house. We moved into the new house and rented out the first house. Years later, we bought two more rental houses.

You'd think it looked like I started beating my wife or something as our friends and family rushed in saying, "What in the world are you doing? Black folks don't do that! That's what White people do."

Even our accountant told us it wasn't a good idea. "You live in a military town," he said. "They're going to shut down the base and the housing market is going to tank." Fear, fear, and more fear.

At one point we had a major expense when an air conditioner broke down on one of the properties. We had money set aside for that kind of event, but people started saying, "What if that happens on more of your properties?" Their fear for us got under our skin after a while.

We were so young and we began to doubt our decision to make those investments. We had a property manager overseeing the tenants, and it was going well, but we listened to the naysayers and ended up selling two of the rental houses. If we hadn't listened to the negaholics, we could have built a good financial nest egg and wealth-building investment for our future. Interest rates were great at that time, and we had more disposable income because we did not have children yet. We could have built it up to twenty rental properties. Instead, we allowed the fearful voices to persuade us.

The Bible says in an abundance of counselors there is victory (Prov. 24:6 NASB). However, "negaholics" (people addicted to negative views of life) don't make good counselors, especially when they have no experience whatsoever in the area they're inserting themselves into. They may have some knowledge, but if they're operating in fear or coming from a place of how the community has always done things, they can't offer good advice. We need to choose our counselors carefully.

As we got older and matured in our relationship with each other and in our faith, many of our friends and family stayed in the same place. They've gotten older, but they haven't grown in wisdom. The definition of wisdom is "the soundness of an action or decision with regard to the application of experience, knowledge, and good judgment." However, Sheila and I incorporate God's principles into that definition. Again, that used to be the norm in generations past, regardless of race.

Over time, Sheila and I have become careful about who we let into our inner circle.

I wanted to grow in my faith. Despite the counsel of family and friends, I learned that once I became courageous in one sense, I had courage in other ways and discovered strength to ignore the negaholics and stay true to my convictions.

When Sheila and I found a church in Tulsa, like Tony Evans' church in Dallas, it happened to have a congregation of 500 people who did not look like us. They were all White. We faced the scourge and ridicule of our family and friends, but I didn't care. We love our family and friends, but we wanted to grow in our faith, and I wasn't willing to compromise my convictions to stay in my cultural comfort zone. My point is, I was more willing to attend a White church that taught scripture than to invest my time in a church that's more of a social club with limited depths of biblical teaching and spiritual growth.

As I mentioned before, Sheila and I also attended Family Life marriage conferences hosted by Dennis and Barbara Rainey and their staff. Sometimes, being in the conference room of 600 people who were not Black helped us gain even more confidence to do things outside the cultural norm and focus on why we attended the conference in the first place—to strengthen our marriage and grow closer together. By that time, it had become normal for us to be the only or one of the few Black couples around.

Sheila and I viewed those marriage conferences as being like a tune-up on our car. If we didn't step outside our daily activities, we never had a chance to tune up our marriage. Being cognizant of my wife is not a firsthand, automatic response for me, especially having been a product of a broken home. The three-day excursions were exactly what we needed every three to five years when we had small kids and I was traveling regularly for work. We always invited family and friends to join us, but to no avail. The weekends were fun and helped strengthen our marriage. We never would have found that kind of resource if we had attended the traditional Black churches we grew up in.

When we went to those events, we didn't know who would be there or what the racial mix would be. Nobody we knew ever attended them. None of our friends or family ever went. When we invited married family members to join us there, they declined, saying didn't want to spend the time or money.

So many people get stuck in how things are "always done." They rationalize why they don't go because "we don't talk about our marriages with strangers." To me, it seemed like the potential depth of relationship they could have was lost. No change, no growth. Forty years later, they're still the same. They missed out on vibrant, life-giving relationships because they listened to voices of the past.

Because of those seminars and the Bible teaching churches, Sheila and I compliment and strengthen each other. Our vertical relationship with God is the basis of our marriage and the thread that makes us strong. Even if we have to speak some hard truths to each other, we deliver them in love. As our marriage has been strengthened, we've become more and more confident to stand up to the voices of the well-meaning negaholics in our lives.

## DISCERNMENT AND COURAGE NEEDED

When someone says something positive, it encourages me to do something proactive. That's how people influence each other. Negaholics have the same emotional effect as when someone cheers me on, only in a disempowering way. If someone says something that reinforces my own negative thinking, I feel comfortable in that space.

I've been told ever since I was a kid that "White people don't like you, you'll never get ahead, they're discriminatory." If I had listened to those voices, they would have pulled me down to the point of giving up. I would have stopped trying. Unfortunately, that's where a lot of the Black community is these days, and it was made worse by political agendas with negative influence over us.

As I referenced before, in the late 1960s, approximately 80 percent of Black children were raised in two-parent families. Today, in nearly every major city, 80 percent of Black children are raised in fatherless homes.[9] This cultural shift has happened without one national initiative to reverse the trend. The Black church is the one institution that should have led a campaign to reverse it.

Instead, Black pastors failed their community and as a result, we are a culture in crisis. To be fair, it was not all Black pastors. There were some exceptions. However, the decline of two-parent families to the lowest levels of any culture in the world has happened on the watch of pastors in these communities. That's why our organization, TakeCharge, is launching a nationwide initiative, inviting leaders and organizations to join our effort to reverse the trend of marriage in the Black community to restore the two-parent household. We call this

---

9    https://www.washingtonexaminer.com/77-black-births-to-single-moms-49-for-hispanic-immigrants

initiative the Prodigal Project. Our hope is that it begins a broader movement outside the Black community and has a positive impact by increasing marriage and reversing the trend to marry later in life.

During the worst of times in American history, from post-Civil War, to Jim Crow, to Redlining (an unethical and unlawful discriminatory practice of systematic denial of services to a certain race or ethnic group), the Black community was comprised mostly of families with a father and a mother. These communities were anchored in our cultural roots of faith, family, and a better education for our children.

Unfortunately, with the dawn of the welfare age, Black pastors did not sound the warning bell loud enough. There were some exceptions, but unfortunately, those exceptions were ignored or drowned out.

Former President Linden Banes Johnson's Great Society social welfare programs in the 1960s financially incentivized women to have children outside of marriage for the first time in U.S. history. The programs were heavily marketed in urban communities. The absence of a husband and father seemed a small price to pay for "free money" and housing. Talk about negative messages!

Sadly, pastors did not band together to warn women about the short and long-term dangers of government dependency, nor did they advise Black men about their responsibilities to their wives and children. Politicians and leaders in the Black community happily got our people hooked on welfare dependency.

Booker T. Washington said, "A lie doesn't become truth, wrong doesn't become right, and evil doesn't become good, just because it's accepted by a majority."[10]

The health of our community reveals the spiraling decline. Based on CDC annual reports:

- Homicide is the number one cause of death for Black male pediatric patients.
- Black Americans rank number one in diabetes.
- Black Americans are number one in obesity.

Although we are only 12 percent of the population, we make up most cases of STDs and most new cases of HIV.

In addition to the destruction of our families, public schools in Black communities are failing our children. In many urban schools, over 60 percent of graduates cannot read, do math, or comprehend science at grade level.

If the Black community is ever to be restored, it will require us to come together under the banner of Jesus Christ and stop listening to the negaholics that would keep us disempowered.

Unfortunately, the White population is now headed where the Black community was back in the '60s. Politicians and government officials are pushing the same narrative to White people that they pushed to Blacks back then. If people are dependent on the government and schools that do not provide a good education and critical thinking skills, the population becomes easier to

---

10   https://quotefancy.com/quote/2360057/Booker-T-Washington-A-lie-doesn-t-become-truth-wrong-doesn-t-become-right-and-evil-doesn

control. The people are forced to need government in their lives because their families are broken. As a result, they will trade their freedom for security.

It's no accident that I'm living in Minnesota, the epicenter of the racial drama we've seen in this country over the past two years. What happened to George Floyd was wrong, no matter how you look at it. It became a political conversation in which the entire White population in America was labeled racist. You'd think we were living in the 1930s with the way the media has been promoting a woefully false, and conveniently consistent, narrative across the network spectrum.

I am not a native of Minnesota. My company, at the time, relocated me and my family here a few years before the riots of 2020 occurred. Like many others, we were chasing the American dream with my career. However, based on my circumstances and my faith, we adjusted our lives to God's plan and purpose. My wife and I made Minnesota our adopted home state. We fell in love with it because we saw a future in which our children could raise their children in an economically thriving area in the beautiful Midwest. I am certain God put us here for a reason and that He has been preparing me throughout my life for what I have begun to do on the path He has put me on.

Miracles only happen when things get so bad that something must change. We don't even recognize miracles when circumstances are good. It's times like these that cause people to rise up and create change.

People from the Black community of the Twin Cities have been joining our organization every month because we stand for bold truth. We are unafraid and casting a vision that they want to be a part of. We receive emails every week asking if we have started a chapter in Nashville, Los Angeles, Houston, Dallas, Atlanta, and many other cities. A woman from Memphis, Tennessee, who showed interest in being a part of TakeCharge, said she felt a lot of resentment toward White people after the George Floyd incident. But she started looking around at the places where she interacted with White people, at work and school, and she realized they didn't treat her the way she had been told White people treated Blacks. In fact, they treated her with professionalism and affection. They were sincere and helpful to people less fortunate than themselves. So, instead of listening to negative messages, she chose to start thinking for herself.

The wrong voices can stop us from stepping out in the direction God has for us. When we oppose the status quo, we become a target for ridicule. I'm not concerned about the naysayers that come after me. My confidence is not in myself but in God and His plan.

The biggest challenge is to take that one step forward. When we demonstrate courage and leadership it encourages others to stand up and step forward. When I speak to people, the issues are related to what is right and wrong and what is best for children and families, regardless of ethnicity. These issues are cultural, not political. We are dealing with issues of right and wrong, good and evil. They are dressed up as issues of racism or politics.

Negaholics can hold us imprisoned in a paradigm that will keep us and our families from flourishing. The first step in taking our power back is to stop listening to naysayers. With discernment and courage, we can bring restoration and healing to the Black community as well as begin a broader, back-to-basics movement that spans beyond racial identity.

# 9: An Uncommon Path to Leadership

After my honorable discharge from the Army, I signed on to be a mentor in the Big Brothers Big Sisters program, which provides one-to-one mentoring relationships that support the critical, social, and emotional development needed to help build resilience and promote the mental health and well-being of thousands of children across America.

Every time we relocated for my job, I got involved with that program. I saw the value in it because I had lived the life those kids are living. They feel like nobody cares about them, they're worthless, and their lives don't matter. I know what that feels like. I wanted to give those kids a masculine role model that I didn't have when I was growing up. I wanted to help them see they are worthy and their past doesn't have to determine their future.

Sheila and I also adopted one of our five children because we believed in living out our faith and being a part of the solution in the Black community. I loved mentoring, but after a while I realized I could only reach one kid at a time. My attempts were useless and I became disheartened. I was only scratching the surface and dealing with the symptoms of the problem rather than the deeper root of it. I came to realize the problem had grown so large that only God could bring about the radical change needed for Black Americans. I prayed that God would intervene and restore Black families and our country. That was more than twenty years ago, and I had no idea then that He would use me to help transform our community in a prodigal-like project.

Looking back on it now, it is amazing to see how God prepared me for this moment. My leadership training began in the U.S. Army Reserves when I was nineteen years old and only a junior in college. Once I graduated from college, I served for a while on active-duty and then I was promoted. As a twenty-three-year-old First Lieutenant, I was responsible for the battalion's tactical nuclear weapons deployment if we ever received the decoded call from the President of the United States. This role required not just a Top-Secret clearance, but a Special Top-Secret clearance. Of the twenty lieutenants in my battalion, the job was given to me by the battalion commander, a lieutenant colonel. It was a big role for someone so young. Thankfully, we never got the call to deploy nuclear weapons.

Every year we had an IG (Inspector General) inspection. The IG inspected every unit to determine if the troops were combat ready and mission capable. It was like a test. Can they maneuver, can they shoot, can they execute? My battalion did fine, but the tactical nuclear team that I led was evaluated separately, and we had the highest marks.

After my promotion to captain, my next assignment was in South Korea leading a team in support of a Tank Battalion. At the end of my assignment in Korea, I decided to leave the Army for a civilian career. I'd had a successful military career, but I wouldn't call it exceptional. By that I mean I wasn't deployed to combat zones multiple times like today's heroes who served. There were no shots fired at me and I never fired a shot at anyone else. I completed my time in the Army with an honorable discharge and a wealth of leadership experiences and exposures from around the world.

During my five years as an officer, I worked with top tier leaders that also elevated my leadership capabilities. It is analogous to competitive sports. Players compete at a higher level when they play opponents that are equal or better than they are.

## CORPORATE LEADERSHIP

After my time in the Army, a Fortune 100 company recruited me. Over the course of my career, I noticed many people had leadership titles even though they didn't possess any leadership traits. The most successful leaders in the corporate world are competent in their field of expertise, good listeners, trustworthy, results-oriented, and they inspire people to achieve beyond their own self-perceptions.

Leaders recruit people that elevate everyone on their teams, including the hiring manager. In fact, you can tell the quality of a leader by watching their hiring decisions and who they have on their direct staff. I hired people based on their capabilities, past successes, and a desire to win. As I mentioned, I like to call them "PhDs," poor, hungry, and determined, because of their strong work ethic and desire to excel. I appreciate competency, but I don't like working with people who are entitled or high maintenance. Unfortunately, the trait of trustworthiness is difficult to glean in the interview process, and I have been burned on occasion with my direct hires.

I once hired a young woman who had quit college to go into real estate. She did that for a while, then went back to finish her degree. When she interviewed with my company for a sales job, I hired her. Over the next several months, I realized she wasn't doing the job she was trained to do. She was taking shortcuts and easy outs with her customers. On one occasion, I accompanied her during sales calls, and when we had a break, I asked what she was doing. She said she was making calls, and she mentioned other busy work.

"That's not how you were trained to do the job," I said. "I want you to stop what you're doing, go home, and re-read the clinical study that we were all assigned to read. The results and data are highly relevant, and you need to make sure you discuss the important findings with the physicians so they have that information. And drop the small talk."

She was taken aback when I told her to meet me in the office at 7:30 in the morning the next day. Weeks later, an opportunity arose to submit her name for a promotion that she was keenly interested in. I didn't give it to her because she hadn't met expectations in her current role. A few months later I received a promotion to the home office, so I was unable to monitor her progress. Six months into my new role, I received a note from her saying she had been upset and angered by what I did, but she realized I was trying to help her be better than she thought she could be.

"Thank you for your support and for pushing me to be better," she wrote. "I qualified for the national sales award this year because you pushed me to better than I thought I could be, and I'm going to Tokyo, Japan, as part of the President's Winner's Circle.

I was so glad she grasped the reason I had approached her the way I did. When you raise your hand to be a leader, you must be willing to be misunderstood, criticized, opposed, accused, and even rejected. I was no longer her manager and wasn't there to see her be successful and go on to win. But I knew she had great potential, and I was happy to see her live up to it.

I enjoyed my new role in the home office where I had a chance to develop the innovative and creative side of my talents. Before the Internet was widely used, no one had websites, and personal email addresses where not common, my company had an innovative new medication that was far superior to that of the market leader in its category. My job in marketing was to help educate our customer base, the market, and ensure the sales force had the training and support needed to increase market share. I decided to explore how the Internet could be a resource in our efforts to differentiate our product and gain additional market visibility.

In 1998, very few medical centers, hospitals, and especially doctors' offices, had their own websites. I was approached by a startup tech company that built websites for businesses. I had them build a website for one segment of our customer base with one caveat: the customer had to include the logo of our product at the bottom of their website in a prominent font. Within a few months, our market share increased significantly, to the point that we surpassed the market leader within a year.

That initial group of specialists, urologists, was the first contingent of medical providers that had websites for their practices before any other medical group in the country. It was so effective that my company asked me to go to Europe and Latin America to train the team there how to launch similar projects.

Leaders often have to step out and try new approaches that have never been tried before. They often fail, but the results can be glorious when they work. A few years later, that program was discontinued. Although it was cleared by our internal legal review team, they shut it down based on where the market was heading with e-healthcare, e-commerce, and tech industry.

## FACILITATING CHANGE

When I ran for Congress in 2020, people were talking about how bad the racial disparities are in America. But the examples they provided are not a result of racial discrimination. The issues are a result of fatherless homes. I'm not talking about broken homes and divorced parents. I'm talking about generations of children who have never had a father.

For example, we interviewed Brandon Tatum of the *Officer Tatum Radio Show*, and he said before he got married, he dated four women at different times and none of them had fathers in their lives. Five generations of Black Americans have lived without a father in the framework of the family. It wasn't always like that, but that has become the norm today. That issue is driving the disparities and the frequent problems Black youth have with the criminal justice system we see today.

Without fathers, there are no grandfathers, no uncles, and no male influence for children to emulate. Remember, this issue of fatherless homes transpired in our lifetimes without one national initiative to reverse the trend. I call it a cultural genocide. We've always looked at these issues with a perspective of what the government can do to help.

When people asked me what I could do if I was elected to Congress, I said, "We don't need government to solve this problem. We need leadership!"

After the election was over and I didn't prevail, I chose to establish TakeCharge, an organization committed to supporting the notion that the promise of America is available to everyone, regardless of race or social station. We believe we own our future by instilling the idea of taking charge of our lives, our families, and our communities. The concept for TakeCharge had been on my heart for at least twenty years. Sheila and I had talked about it throughout most of our marriage.

It's not a political movement. It is a "doing what is right movement." Again, it's analogous to the prodigal son realizing that he veered far from beliefs and values he was taught while suffering from the poor decisions he made. The son realizes his mistake and earnestly returns to his father, hoping to work as one of his servants.

At TakeCharge, we are working to get the attention of the people who, like the prodigal son, are stuck in the muck of their bad decisions. We aim to help them realize there is a better way, returning their hearts and minds back to the teaching of God. Our message is simple, but the journey will not be easy. We emphasize a three-fold return to:

1) Faith (the teaching of God and his Son, Jesus Christ found in the Holy Bible)
2) Family (the traditional two-parent nuclear family)
3) Education (securing a better education for our children which includes school choice options)

The notion behind TakeCharge is for people to take responsibility for their life, their family, and their community. We don't need government grants. We don't need free money. We don't need permission from any politician to thrive. And we don't need any new laws established, other than school choice options, to make this transformation.

At TakeCharge, we encourage kids to graduate from high school, get a job, get married, then have children, in that order. Not in reverse.

We are attracting people from the Black community who realize the truth but never had a platform to express their viewpoints. Our volunteers don't get interviewed by the legacy press because our message doesn't fit their narrative. A large part of the Black community has no public voice and no advocates for their values, so we provide that for them. We have the largest number of Black Americans who denounce critical race theory (CRT) and Black Lives Matter (BLM), and we are outspoken about the need to get back to the basics of faith, family, and education.

From a faith perspective, the premises of Black Lives Matter and critical race theory are anti-God, anti-family, and anti-American values. Both of those organizations have political agendas and neither of them have Black people's best interest in mind. They have duped a vast majority of Americans and Black Americans. BLM has recently been exposed for raising millions of dollars and not using any of it for the purposes they originally promised it would be used for. CRT is nothing more than a political movement using racial strife to push their political agenda. That includes the Diversity Equity Inclusion (DEI) agenda.

Sadly, the church today has shied away from the truth about the fatherless home crisis, and it is spreading beyond the Black community into society in general, to the detriment of our country. Cancel culture has not only censored Christians but it has also caused us to silence ourselves. A large portion of our nation's churches are AWOL on this issue and many more.

When we launched TakeCharge, I went into the Black community and started talking to people. Every month we welcome more and more volunteers from the Black community. None of those people are compensated, but all of them want to return the Black culture to its historical norms and help facilitate change. They are working for the sake of young Black kids, to instill faith in God in them, and to show them how to flourish in life.

We began TakeCharge in 2020, and I took a hiatus to run as a candidate for Governor during half that year. I'm amazed at the traction we've had in such a short time. There are millions of people outside the Black community who want to see Black people and their families do well. You'll never hear that in any mainstream news outlets or from American university administrators, but these people want Black families to do well. They're generous with their time and money and have been for decades.

I recently received a text from one Black man saying he had been stuffing the memories and feelings of his traumatic childhood down for most of his life, and that he wants to be a part of what we're doing. Besides him, we get texts and emails on a daily basis from people around the country who want to get involved with our mission.

We've had to tell some potential volunteers to wait until we get our programs in place so they can serve as coaches, mentors, and marriage counselors. I feel honored to work with the people who are willing to be vulnerable and share their lives for one objective: to turn the tide for Black children and families.

## SURVIVING VERSUS THRIVING

Because we have allowed five generations of Black children to grow up without fathers, we are toxic in our own communities and in the public square with fellow Americans. We're like ticking time bombs. The deep-seated hurt and anger manifests in how we treat others within our community and those in the broader culture.

Unfortunately, our policies at the state and federal level undermine strong families and weaken the foundation of our country. Our government policies are incentivizing the wrong behaviors. Marriage and families strengthen societies and are the best environment in which to raise children. If we accept government assistance for the roof over our heads, food on our tables, cell phones and childcare, we inadvertently surrender our freedom.

I created TakeCharge because the cultural landscape has become so bad that pastors are not even addressing the issues. I don't preach, and I'm not a "Bible thumper," but I do believe we are called to stand up against evil and to show the way for people who are lost.

One of our volunteers at TakeCharge grew up believing marriage was meaningless at best, because that's what the Black community has been led to believe. She never saw the value in being married, even though she had four children from the man she'd been living with, until she started helping at TakeCharge. When she got involved with us, I didn't pressure her about being unmarried. She came to her decision on her own.

One day she said, "If I'm going to be a mentor, I need to walk the talk." She and her boyfriend didn't even tell me they were going to get married. They had a private wedding ceremony. Later, she mentioned that one of her friends in her mid-thirties said she had never been to a wedding before. Their marriage felt like the beginning of the cultural change we want to see.

## CASTING A VISION

Sheila and I were asked to speak at an event in Louisiana in 2021. We stayed at a nice hotel where a bellman, an older Black gentleman, smiled as he met us at the front door. As we approached, he leaned toward me and said, "You're going to speak in front of millions. And you're going to sit around a table with millionaires and billionaires."

I didn't think much of it. He didn't know me, so how could he predict such a thing anyway? This was a year before I ran for governor.

However, now with TakeCharge alone, I literally have millionaires and billionaires coming alongside to help us. They see what we are trying to do and they are now personal friends of ours. I say this not to brag, but to show that people are seeing the value in what we are doing and that God brings the resources to his people who are faithful and courageous.

When people see the authenticity, they are drawn to what we're doing. They want to be a part of it and help with it. People want to contribute to something that makes a difference, something dynamic and life-changing that creates peace, harmony, and goodwill in the world. They want to be on a winning team, not one that is dividing families and tearing down humanity. We can all sit around and complain as we watch our society crumble under woke agendas, or we can be a force for good.

Minneapolis became the epicenter of rioting and looting after the death of George Floyd, and it spread across the country in the summer of 2020. It is my prayer and vision to see Minneapolis known for something quite different, the city where the two-parent family was resurrected. TakeCharge is now a grassroots movement in the Twin Cities. It is made up of mothers, fathers, and grandparents from the Black community as well as the White community. They are modern foot-soldiers committed to returning the Black community to its cultural roots of faith, family, and education.

Leaders must often cast a vision for something that doesn't even exist yet. Their job is to make people want to be a part of it. That's what we're doing with Take Charge.

People often say, "I can't see this happening."

I say, "That's why they call it a miracle."

## GOD'S BIGGER PICTURE

Near the end of 2021, I was encouraged to run for governor of Minnesota. There were seven candidates competing for the Republican nomination for governor of Minnesota in 2022. Two of them had been in the campaign for more than a year. The rest had been in for seven or eight months. I joined in January 2022, so I only had four months to gain visibility before the state endorsement convention.

There was a statewide straw poll (an unofficial vote) for all the delegates. Minnesota holds a delegate endorsement convention every election year, followed by a primary in August. The primary becomes like a wedding ceremony in which a single candidate is selected to represent each party.

I traveled all around Minnesota and met tens of thousands of people across our state of eighty-seven counties. As the campaign moved along, people became excited about my candidacy and message. In October of 2009, *Forbes Magazine* surveyed twenty-five major cities in the United States and ranked Minneapolis as the safest city and best quality of life.

By 2021, homicides and car jackings were completely out of control. I pledged to restore the Twin Cities to its normative state within twenty-four months. I also pledged to return public schools to basic education and perform a major tax overhaul for the state. However, the major appeal of my candidacy was my personal story of achievement from the ghettos of Harlem and a trailer park in Oklahoma. My heart of gratitude provided people with a sense of hope and inspiration.

Three months before the endorsement convention, a poll was taken in Chisago county. Out of seven candidates, I moved from last place to second place behind the lead candidate, Scott Jensen. I then moved from fourth place to second state-wide. During one of the last straw polls, people said they would never elect a Black man in the rural areas of the state, but the fact that I kept climbing in the top tier of candidates tells me most Americans have gotten past that opinion.

At the convention, 2,200 delegates decide who will be the endorsed candidate. If a candidate doesn't get enough delegates, they must drop out. Then they are expected to endorse others who are still in. At the start of the convention, the first-round votes revealed Scott Jensen had 26 percent of the delegate votes and I had 23 percent. The remaining candidates were far behind. After two state senators dropped out and endorsed my candidacy, I was propelled into the number one position but didn't have enough votes to secure the nomination of the convention of delegates.

By the sixth round of votes, it looked like I would get the Republican nomination. However, the third remaining candidate came to my "war room" to negotiate a deal in exchange for his endorsement, which would put me over the top. He said he would endorse me if I agreed to choose him as my running mate for lieutenant governor. I told him no, and I offered him a different position that I thought he would be better suited for. He was offended at my offer, so he marched on stage in front of the entire convention, called me a sell-out and a liar, and had a surrogate do the same. He then endorsed Scott Jensen, who won the endorsement nomination as the Republican candidate for Governor. Scott Jensen ultimately lost in the November election to his Democratic opponent, Minnesota Governor Tim Walz.

## Character Has More Influence Than Rank

I was never looking to become a politician, nor do I need a political title to make a difference for our communities. I got involved in the gubernatorial race primarily to reverse the trend of violence in our state, provide school choice options for parents, and improve the economic climate to reverse the exodus of people leaving Minnesota.

Since the election, my focus has been on expanding the mission at TakeCharge. I want our nonprofit organization to grow so big and so effective that I can't take time to run for office again in the future. If I can help the Black community turn a corner with TakeCharge, perhaps we will have a cascading effect across the country.

We all know the biblical story of how a shepherd boy named David slayed the giant, Goliath. Yet we often forget the details about the story of King David. When he was anointed king by the prophet Samuel, the crown was not placed on his head at that time. The crown came more than ten years later, after much hardship and threats to his life. David never complained about his path to the throne. Likewise, Moses and Joseph each experienced hard times before they were recognized as leaders. Many years passed before God used them for his purposes.

I am trusting in God to work in me like he did in David and Joseph. My leadership training, my experience in the military, and my corporate career set me up to do what I'm doing now. I believe there is a picture forming that I cannot see now. I trust in God's plan and timing for what he has in store, and it may or may not include political office.

# 10: A New Breed of Superhero

Coming out of my childhood situation and my parents' divorce, I had nobody to go to for support. My mom was too far away, and my father was all discipline and no empathy. I was never homeless, but I sure know what it's like to feel abandoned. As I mentioned previously, I volunteered with the Big Brothers Big Sisters organization as a young adult. I found it so rewarding that since then, I have been a huge advocate of mentoring. I admire people who give of their time, wisdom, and resources to help those who are less fortunate.

My first mentorship with Big Brothers was in Dallas. The first little brother I was assigned to was Trey Ellis, a young man who needed a male figure in his life. At eleven or twelve years old, he was playing baseball and his coach said he had anger issues. Trey and I talked at length about stuff he was going through and about what had him feeling so angry. His father was

Dock Ellis, a major league baseball pitcher for the Pittsburgh Pirates and later, the Texas Rangers.

Dock Ellis struggled with substance abuse, which short-circuited his career and possibly triggered the divorce from Trey's mother. I was Trey's big brother for a year before my job transferred me away from Dallas. It broke my heart to leave Trey after we had established a strong rapport, and he cried. It grieved me because Trey had a distant relationship with his father and suddenly I was leaving his life.

I followed up with Trey through Facebook a few years ago and was delighted to discover he remembered me. He had been playing basketball in the NBA for a short time, finished college, and he is now a teacher at a school in California. I was so happy to know he made choices that led him in a good direction. In other words, he didn't go wrong. He's a young man living a successful life.

Some kids, because of their home environment, are forced to make adult decisions at an early age when they're not equipped to do so. But it only takes one or two good choices to get someone to head in the right direction. Poverty can be eradicated in one generation based on making the right choices. Having responsible adults in a child's life helps them make better decisions.

I met a man a few years ago who mentored an immigrant from homelessness to college education. His story reminded me of the *Blind Side* movie. He and his wife took in a young man who had no place to go and raised him like a surrogate son. The kid was originally from Africa and didn't speak English. They helped him learn the language and complete high school. They then paid for his first year of college, after which he received scholarships for the remaining three years. He is now living a prosperous life in America because someone stepped up to help him. I've noticed that when Americans see someone trying to better their lot in life, their first inclination is to help.

Sheila and I know a retired couple who are spending their retirement years helping inner city teens prepare for the ACT test to give them a better chance of being accepted into college. They spend every Saturday working with the kids for several hours at a time, and they don't charge a single dime for their service. In my mind, those who step up to mentor are a new breed of superhero. They are unsung heroes in our society that the media rarely highlights.

## DEDICATION, PASSION, AND CALLING

Another friend of ours came to faith in God in his forties and decided he would follow what he believed God was telling him to do. Jeff Bird felt called to start Hope Academy, a top-notch college prep school for inner city kids. In doing so, he moved his family from a nice neighborhood in suburban Minneapolis to an old historic house in downtown Minneapolis. It's a nice home though it's in "the hood," literally just a couple of blocks from where George Floyd died and where the riots of 2020 started.

Hope Academy is a private, Christ-centered, classical academy founded as an opportunity-equalizer for urban youth. Jeff and his wife, Widdy, opened the school twenty years ago with seventy kids. They now have 700 students, many of them Black and Hispanic, and the kids attend for little to no cost. Under the Birds' mentorship, the students graduate from high school. Compared to what they would have had in the Minneapolis public school system, they have a new start in life, simply because Jeff followed the vision God gave him.

Several years ago, Jeff began receiving calls from school counselors about kids falling through the cracks in public middle school and high school. Many of them were reading two to three grade levels behind. Heading into high school, the students are expected to catch up after being left behind in elementary schools. Jeff says it's like driving a model T and trying to accelerate up the onramp to catch up with traffic going seventy miles per hour.

Jeff and Widdy responded to the call for help by starting a second program called Hope Farm School. Through this program, located on 400 acres, they help underprivileged boys graduate from high school while teaching them life skills they were never taught at home. They teach them how to get up on time in the morning and do chores such as tending to cows, chickens, and crops.

The boys meet at Jeff's house in downtown Minneapolis every Sunday night and he drives them out to the farm in a big yellow bus. It takes an hour and a half to get there, even longer on icy roads in the middle of winter. Jeff spends the night at the farm, then gets up and goes to his day job on Monday mornings. The students live in a bunkhouse on the farm five days a week, along with a dozen or so staff members and residence assistants. They learn math, science, and economics through hands-on activities of raising crops, selling produce, selling beef, and seeing the return they get for their labor. The farm school has two teachers on staff, but the academic part is the easy part.

Teaching the kids practical life skills, such as showing up to work on time and working with a good attitude, is the challenging part. Some of the inner-city kids cuss at them, yet Jeff and Widdy stick with the boys until they've processed their anger and become more amiable. At Hope Farm School, they learn respect and responsibility, literally life-changing skills they will benefit from for the rest of their lives.

Teenagers in healthy two-parent homes sometimes have bad attitudes, but the farm kids have never had any boundaries. Most of the boys come from hurting families and single-parent homes. They've been abused and seen the worst of American society, and initially, they bring all that with them to the farm. Many inner-city minority youth face difficult challenges due to negative influences, difficult living environments, and failing schools. They also are often missing a positive fatherly influence. All these factors combine for a high school graduation rate well below 50 percent, and poor prospects for their life.

Jeff grew up on a farm in Iowa, and this school was never in his career agenda or retirement plan. He and Widdy are in their sixties now. They could be retired and living in Florida, but their dedication, passion, and faith keep them focused on pouring into the kids' lives. They are committed to changing the environment for inner-city children, removing them from negative influences, and helping them receive positive, godly guidance.

Thanks to Jeff and Widdy Bird, these young men are living like Americans lived a century ago, when America was an agrarian society. They are exposed to an economy based on producing and maintaining crops and farmland.

Some of the boys go on to college, and one of them recently got a full-ride scholarship to a local college. One Hispanic student graduated high school and went into construction work. When he got married, three generations of family and friends attended the ceremony. None of them had ever been to a wedding before.

Mentoring one child can have an impact on an entire community, but it is only meant to fill a gap in a child's life and in society. It's not meant to be the complete program. Two-parent families are supposed to be the primary program, and unfortunately, they are the exception. Broken homes and neglected children are so prevalent that many kids are fortunate if they do have a mentor. These kids would have been left behind and likely ended up as statistics in our criminal justice system if it wasn't for this program.

When I think I want to pat myself on the back for things I've done, I think of Jeff and Widdy Bird, and I'm humbled. They have six children of their own, two of whom they adopted from Ethiopia. I have been so impressed with the work they do that I enrolled my son in the farm school for his senior year. They easily qualify as superheroes in my book.

## TURNING THE CULTURE AROUND

There are people in need everywhere, but they need much more than an occasional handout or a free meal. They need more than prayer. They need action. Kids need a stable life with a mom and a dad, and so many don't have that. In the United States, we have no promotional activity and no educational foundation promoting marriage before children. Our society doesn't encourage two-parent families. Our political environment actually discourages it.

A study conducted on kids who have done some of the recent school shootings revealed that most of the youth fit the same profile of male, broken family, no father in the home.[11]

A recent school shooting in Dallas was perpetrated by a Black teen who said, "No one cares about me. I have no mother, no father. No one cares."

I don't mean to generate sympathy for that boy, but when that central foundation of child rearing is off kilter, the symptoms of those problems show up in our public arenas.

I am a proponent of marriage and two-parent families, but that doesn't mean I am anti anything else. At TakeCharge, our number one priority is to reverse the complete breakdown of the Black family, not only in the Black community, but across the country because it is spreading to other communities as well. Other data shows that kids prosper academically, socially, and economically when they grow up in a traditional, nuclear family.[12]

I started hearing the phrase White privilege and systemic racism about four years ago. It struck me as absurd. White priv-

---

11  Farrell, Warren. *The Boy Crisis: Why our boys are struggling and what we can do about it.* BenBella Books, 2018.

12  https://journals.sagepub.com/doi/abs/10.1177/019251394015001006

ilege and systemic racism were issues my parents and grandparents dealt with when they lived in the Jim Crow South. These were not problems of our era since the 1970s. My parents would have loved to have grown up in the America I grew up in. We rarely talk about the progress we have made since that era. Politicians, academia, and news media never make the distinction that 90 percent of the disparities we face today can be attributed to the generational welfare dependency that was created in the mid-1960s and early 1970s.

The narrative we have about systemic racism is completely fabricated. I discerned that the narrative was a propaganda machine for a political agenda, and I felt obligated to step forward and do something. As I mentioned previously, I got involved in the public arena because there are stories about people all over the country who have stepped up to help others, especially kids, who don't look like them. They do it out of the goodness of their hearts, out of their obedience to their faith, and they don't seek any recognition for it at all.

Love doesn't know skin color. Compassion doesn't know skin color. We shouldn't disparage people who are willing to open their lives and homes to people who don't look like they do. If we have the capacity in our life to help, we would do well to assist someone who is struggling.

In America, we now have five generations that have been trained in the welfare dependency that has destroyed the God-given motivation we have for life. Because of this indoctrination, we now have countless people who are constantly in need. We've allowed the absence of fathers, grandfathers, and wise sages to become normative, to our own detriment. Leaders in the progressive movement use this cycle of disparity and hopelessness as an example of systemic racism even though they know it is a lie. They use crisis for their political agendas.

Before I became a Christian, I was not looking to be involved in church and I wasn't looking for God. I believed in God, but I didn't believe the church as I knew it was relevant for my life. I realized later that the church as I knew it was not the church that God intended for his followers.

As I mentioned earlier, I started attending Tony Evans' church in Dallas when I first became a Christian. I took their new member class on what it meant to be a member of the church and a Christian. The teaching helped me unlearn old paradigms and then learn that church is not intended to be an entertainment venue or a bless-me club. That's not what church is about, regardless of what is taught in other churches. Jesus came to serve and to be a light in a dark world. His followers are called to serve and to be a light as well. The class taught me that nobody should be sitting in the stands like spectators. I had never heard that in a Black church. I imagine most people sitting in that class had never heard it either.

They also told us if we wanted to attend church as a couple, we needed to be married. "We don't do shack-ups here," they said. They didn't mean to shame anyone, but if a couple is living together, the expectation is to be living in holy matrimony as God designed. That was a radical idea to me at the time. It was unheard of in the churches I grew up in, and it's not mentioned in today's churches either. Today's pastors seem to lack the courage to speak up about biblical standards of behavior.

The Twin Cities in Minnesota have more than one hundred nonprofit organizations. That's probably the case in every major city in the country. Very few of them encourage young people to get married before having children, but that is that is how the cycle of poverty could be stopped. I'm convinced there is a segment of American society that doesn't want that dependent behavior to change. There are people and organizations benefitting from poor and ignorant people being held prisoner in the system of poverty and dependency.

But I say it is possible to turn the tide of poverty and ignorance in one generation. Anyone can help lift someone else out of hopelessness by showing up and investing time in them.

Another volunteer family recently joined us at TakeCharge. The husband, Tom, had grown up in a poor family in a drug and crime infested part of town. At his father's request, he used to visit a man who lived in an apartment upstairs. The man would always ask him to deliver small packages to other people in the neighborhood. He never questioned the activity because he trusted his father and, by extension, trusted his father's friend. At one point, his mother discovered Tom was delivering drugs unknowingly, and she quickly moved the family to a new location away from that activity.

While in high school, Tom played football and wanted to be an NFL football star, but he had a major injury that prevented him from playing further. By his senior year, he had fallen so far behind academically that he wasn't going to graduate. Thankfully, a mentor worked with him and helped him graduate from high school on time. He then got a job, got married, and now he has four children who are doing well. He and his wife Cecilia are each working good jobs.

Cecilia was one of six kids, and all her siblings have different fathers. It's strange to imagine growing up with such a revolving door of men, but Cecilia and Tom were able to break the cycle because they got together and declared they would not live like the families they grew up in. Now their children are living in a stable, two-parent, hard-working family. They are holding it together, and their children will have a completely different life than they had. That's how poverty can be overcome in one generation.

Tom's father recently came to the faith and had an instant change. He stopped drinking and doing drugs and he reconnected with his family. Since then, the family has enjoyed restorative healing and growth.

We have more than a dozen couples involved with Take-Charge that have come from similar backgrounds. They want to help turn the culture around, and they're doing it on their own, at no cost, no compensation, and no personal accolades. They do it because they know how dysfunctional the impoverished communities are. I feel humbled and honored when they share their private stories.

## PAUL AND TIMOTHY

Whenever I hear about someone living a successful, responsible life, I don't have to look far to find a mentor-mentee or a Paul and Timothy kind of relationship. Movies like *The Karate Kid* and *Star Wars* even feature them.

Having someone to look up to and go to for support is one the most important things a kid can have. Mentors give youth, and even some adults, the confidence they need to confront challenges and come up with their own solutions. They provide a safe place for kids and teens to be themselves and learn valuable life skills. Mentors lead by example, showing mentees how to adapt to challenges in life. Mentors inspire students to become leaders.

I am grateful for the Timothies I have mentored in my life. They are my legacy and a large part of the fulfillment I've experienced through the years. I highly recommend finding a Timothy if you don't already have one. Unfortunately, many Americans are consumed with their careers, vacations, and retirement. Many are struggling to keep their own chin above water. They don't see giving time or resources as a component to a rich and rewarding life.

The rewards of serving others who are less fortunate are infinite. The biblical principles of sowing and reaping, as well as giving and receiving, helped me and many others to stop focusing on our own circumstances and move beyond survival. It's counterintuitive, but when we give sacrificially, whether of our time, talents, or money, it's amazing what God does in return.

# 11: Diversity, Equity, and Inclusion

In public schools, large corporate American businesses, and in private and public universities around the country, employees and students are required to participate in diversity and inclusion workshops or seminars. At the end of the training, nearly everyone feels divided, angry, and confused.

The attitude of those presenting this doctrine is, "Tough, too bad, you're White. You're guilty, and people of non-White ethnicity are victims."

In the fall of 2022, I went to hear Nikole Hannah-Jones speak about her work, *The 1619 Project*. She attracted a large audience at the University of Minnesota, and I was curious to know what she had to say.

According to the 1619 education website, *"The 1619 Project* is an anthology of essays edited by Nikole Hannah-Jones and co-created with the *New York Times* that seeks to reframe American history with the institution of slavery at its core. The book asserts that American history began in 1619 with the arrival of the first ship of enslaved Africans, one year before the *Mayflower* arrived. It also argues that American democracy and the prosperous nation we know today were largely built by enslaved Black Americans but that this demographic is almost entirely excluded from America's founding stories and remains suppressed today due to racist institutions that persist from slavery."[13]

Nikole's book asserts that the founders of America wanted to break away from England because they wanted to keep slavery legal. In other words, slavery was the real motivation for establishing a new country, not what has been taught historically. *The 1619 Project* is a distortion of history. Hannah-Jones has even been condemned from leftist historians, but it didn't matter because her message became the framework for the current diversity, equity, and inclusion (DEI) conversation. For those who have embraced her message, this has become their religion, disguised as Critical Race Theory (CRT), or its pseudonym, DEI. It is applied much like the Bible and prayer were used in public schools in the past.

As I listened to Nikole's lecture, she talked about how slavery was bad, Jim Crow was bad, and how all disparities today are based on those historical events. However, she never said anything about the government policies and programs that created the disparities we have in fatherless homes and inner-city gangs. She didn't touch on the underbelly of the leftist policy of Linden Banes Johnson's Great Society social welfare programs.

---

13  https://1619education.org/?gclid=CjwKCAiA-dCcBhBQEiwAeWidtYb5MXjCq
TBmVyzdWymqthwraIR4VsdA24Gm7Ea6dSgqA_BjvJwk2BoCwLoQAvD_BwE

These new programs were heavily marketed in big cities across the country in Black communities, and they introduced something new to the American landscape. For the first time in American history, the federal government financially incentivized women to have children outside of marriage. A variation of that program still exists today. Neither Hannah-Jones nor any other agents of CRT ever mention the program and the destruction of the Black family it has caused.

Nikole mentioned she had a Black father and a White mother. She grew up in Waterloo, Iowa, and her father was a staunch patriot, even though he grew up in segregated Mississippi. He served in the military and flew a big American flag in front of their house. She also stated that her father suffered during Jim Crow segregated laws. However, she did not. Born in 1976, she led a very different life than previous generations. She attended Notre Dame University, where she enrolled in African American studies, a relatively new field of academic study at the time, rooted in socialist and Marxist ideology. As she immersed herself in those classes, she began to hate this country and question her father's patriotism.

After Nikole's hour-long talk, someone asked her how we could find a way forward.

She responded, "Whenever I hear a question like that, what I really hear is 'How do White people get off the hook?'"

She didn't offer any ideas for redemption or reconciliation. She did call for reparations to be made, but how would anyone be able to determine which White people are descendants of slave owners, and which Black people are descendants of their slaves? And who is going to pay for the research and computer programs necessary to match everyone up?

It's ludicrous to say that all White people are responsible for slavery. I wonder about the descendants of White Americans who never had slaves or descendants who died fighting for the Union Army. Some of them never owned slaves and others didn't even arrive in the U.S. until the 1950s. Nikole and her ilk possess an anti-God, anti-American and anti-nuclear family belief system based on socialist ideology. There is never a remediation pathway for them.

Most people don't know that African American studies are rooted in communism.[14] The people behind the communistic trends are experimenting on the nation and our children based on something they believe. Yet they have no evidence of their moral certitudes working anywhere in history. There is no way to measure and calculate their success. If they wanted to see how well it works (or how much damage it does), they could look at what happened to Venezuela. They have pushed their agenda out to the public to the detriment of our society, especially our children.

After listening to Nikole Hannah-Jones speak, it became clear to me that these people don't want racism to go away. Apparently, there is a one-sided benefit to maintaining a culture in crisis.

Many of the African American studies are called "grievance studies" because there is never any reconciliation. There is never

---

14   https://www.peoplesworld.org/article/communists-and-the-long-struggle-for-african-american-equality/

a path forward on which we come together in unity. If there was a path forward, those in power would become irrelevant. The people teaching those studies want everyone to be accepting and tolerant, yet they are intolerant of the Christian values and traditions this country was founded on. The communism part of African American studies and DEI is in direct conflict with the ideals of America. They seem to believe there will be no peace until their system of belief and governance overtakes our liberties and freedoms, including free speech.

As I mentioned before, the driver of this mindset is rooted in a socialist/communist ideology and old fashion greed for power and money. You just read about the power component. The money component can be summed up by a quote from Booker T. Washington.

"There is another class of coloured people who make a business of keeping the troubles, the wrongs, and the hardships of the Negro race before the public. Having learned that they are able to make a living out of their troubles, they have grown into the settled habit of advertising their wrongs, partly because they want sympathy and partly because it pays. Some of these people do not want the Negro to lose his grievances, because they do not want to lose their jobs."[15]

## INCLUSIVE VERSUS EXCLUSIVE
I recently saw that the Kroger grocery chain is preparing to merge with another large grocery company. The Federal Trade

---

15   Washington, Booker T. *Up From Slavery.* 1901.

Commission has been holding a hearing about preventing them from merging because that would make them a huge corporation, bigger than half the grocery stores in the country. The CEO of Kroger was at the meeting asking for help, and Tom Cotton, a U.S. Senator from Arkansas, spoke up and mentioned that Kroger fires employees who refuses to wear rainbow aprons during pride month. Their DEI training states that the terms "sir" and "ma'am" should not be used, all in the name of inclusivity.

Their definition of inclusivity means employees must accept their values and preferences while they are blatantly rejecting the values and preferences of their employees. They are forcing a culture change. How is it inclusive to tell a sixty or seventy-year-old employee, who has been calling people sir or ma'am out of respect all their life, that they'll be reprimanded for using those terms?

In other news, someone proposed taking Christmas off the calendar because it's not inclusive of people who are not Christian. I find that so odd because I don't feel left out of Hanukah or Ramadan.

It's clear to me that inclusivity is being used as a weapon.

According to Webster's Dictionary, *inclusion* means "the act of including: the state of being included."[16] Common sense would say that means including everyone, not just a special group. But some people, in the name of social justice, have stretched that term to mean everyone must adopt the ideologies of one previously marginalized group. I don't have a problem

---

16   https://www.merriam-webster.com/dictionary/inclusion

respecting the choices and values of another person, but I expect them to respect mine, too. It shouldn't be a one-way street.

Government programs, corporations, and activists are not the only ones creating division in the name of inclusivity. Years ago, Maulana Karenga, a convicted felon, created the holiday known as Kwanzaa, supposedly as a way for African American families to reconnect to their roots and to unite as a community. Kwanzaa is exclusively an American holiday. It is not celebrated in any other part of the world (including Africa). The man who created the holiday, Maulana Karenga (born Ronald McKinley Everett), described the 2019 celebration as "an all-seasons celebration and practice of the good." The problem with that statement is that Maulana Karenga is anything but good. He was convicted in 1971 of torturing two women who were members of his separatist organization known as US (United Slaves), a Black nationalist cult he founded.

Kwanzaa is observed from December 26 to January 1 and culminates in gift-giving and a big feast.[17] When he invented the holiday, Karenga said his goal was to "give Blacks an alternative to the existing holiday and give Blacks an opportunity to celebrate themselves and history, rather than simply imitate the practice of the dominant society."

## A BETTER WAY

At TakeCharge, we are taking a stand that reconciliation is possible. As Americans, we can learn and we can get better. We

---

17  https://researchguides.cpcc.edu/winterholidaysandcelebrations/kwanzaa

are not victims and we do not need to subscribe to perpetual victimhood. We can rise from our circumstances. There is a path forward. The children of White slave owners are not guilty of slavery, as Nikole Hannah-Jones suggested, just because their ancestors had slaves.

I firmly believe there is a better way to reconcile our differences. This diversity statement from Biola University says it best:

"From the time of original creation to the redemption of the new creation, God's heart for both diversity and unity is evident. Unlike many efforts which seek to highlight one aspect to the detriment of the other, scripture emphasizes the importance of both diversity and unity (1 Cor. 12:12-13). Unity without diversity ceases to be unity and becomes uniformity, and diversity without unity ultimately becomes either radical tribalism or individualism. Christians are called to pursue diversity and unity differently: not as an either/or, but a both/and."[18]

Our military and professional sports teams have been a wonderful example of that over the last thirty or forty years. Those people all came from diverse backgrounds, but they come together to be successful on the field even though they all have different skill sets, skin color, and economic backgrounds. They set all of that aside to work together for a common good. Even after a football game, the players on the losing team walk around congratulating the players on the winning team. The cameras continue to roll as Black and White players hug each other and shake hands.

---

18   https://www.biola.edu/about/diversity

In the political arena, it used to be common for a candidate who didn't win an election to work with the winner to bring everyone forward in unity. Now the losing side does everything they can to stop the winners, even if it means lie, cheat, and steal to destroy the opposing party. They gleefully support the idea of a resistance movement. Really? Resisting a lawfully elected citizen? When does resistance end and treason begin?

Voices such as TakeCharge and others must get the message out in creative ways because the left and their allies in the media, entertainment, and academia are dominating the primary platforms, including sources that most Americans have trusted for decades. American citizens have always lived in what I call the "sensible center." Unfortunately, those in the sensible center have no idea they are being manipulated toward radical ideologies.

I want to be part of the force that brings Americans back to common sense, individual responsibility, and respect for other people regardless of their differing views. I feel like I've stepped out of *The Matrix* movie and begun looking at the world from a different perspective. I've started to question things. I'm just an ordinary man, but I think if I could take some people on the path I've walked, they would see things differently as well.

Taking charge of my own life put me on a journey of faith, family, education, and benefits of capitalism for creating generational wealth. From that worldview, I can see the alternate worldview of government as the benefactor being pushed and propagandized to the masses through mainstream media, academia, and the entertainment industry.

I'm standing back saying, "Wait a minute! The path I took is the same path as other Americans from different ethnic groups. The path includes getting an education, working hard, having children after getting married, saving and investing money, and faith in God. If they believe their methodologies are beneficial for the masses, where are the results of feasibility studies or pilot programs? They have no thread of evidence.

In the fall of 2022, Elon Musk tweeted a message that I found pertinent to the topic of Reparation. "It is easy to fool people, but it is almost impossible to convince people that they have been fooled."

Progressives and their allies in the Black community have fooled a large percentage of Americans that today's disparities are because of historical racial injustices, White privilege, and systemic racism. They fail to mention the biggest driver of disparities in the Black community was a result of LBJ's Great Society social welfare programs and the surrogates that exist to this very day. When it was introduced, it was the first time in American history that the federal government financially incentivized women to have children outside of marriage. That program was the left's Trojan Horse to create permanent one-party rule in the largest cities in the country and the eventual demise of the Black family.

In 1965, the same time that the Great Society was introduced to the American public, the late Senator of New York Daniel Patrick Moynihan wrote his famous report, "The Negro Family, The Case for National Action." (Before he was Senator, Moynihan worked in the LBJ administration.) In the report he stated, "In a word, a national effort towards the problems of Negro Americans must be directed towards the question of family structure. The object should be to strengthen the Negro family so as to enable it to raise and support its members as do other families." Moynihan and others thought 24 percent of unmarried births in the Black community was a crisis at the time. His recommendations were ignored.

Civil rights leaders who sacrificed for the benefits we have today must be rolling in their graves. This generation of Black leaders ushered in the swap of fathers for the revolving door of baby daddies. Fathers who are present and involved in their children's lives provide discipline, security, and growth. Absent men do not. Leftist arguments of racial, economic, and academic disparities leave out the inconvenient truth of five generations of welfare dependent fatherless homes.

We can see a reversal in the Black community in one generation by returning to cultural roots of faith, family, and education. From a financial perspective, and getting an early start on the turnaround process, we first need to re-introduce vocational education into high schools and prepare students to be workforce-ready upon graduation.

# 12: The Source of Lasting Change

Jason Riley of the *Wall Street Journal* recently wrote, "For the first time in American history, four of the largest cities in our country will be led by Black mayors beginning in 2023. Since 1970, the number of Black elected officials has grown from fewer than 1,500 to more than 10,000. This success is important but does not change a key reality. We have not seen equal progress in economic growth or academic success in the Black community over the same period of time."[19]

From my personal experience and fifty years of national evidence, it is obvious to me that progress for the Black community will not come from politicians or the government. The ideals of America were never designed for people to expect their individual prosperity to come from the government. In the United

---

19   https://www.wsj.com/articles/four-biggest-cities-black-mayors-los-angeles-economic-advancement-voters-minority-ethnic-race-elected-official-11669759694?st=nt2v6vdpxb98jqn&reflink=desktopwebshare_permalink

States, we can rely on ourselves, hard work, education, and principles of capitalism that have lifted millions of people out of poverty. Progress can happen, and it can be done in one generation. However, it takes a dedicated few working together to create transformation toward a new reality.

Politicians are usually fast followers of society's leaders. Historically, lasting change has been initiated by an individual or a small group of people who took a stand.

The civil rights movement was a struggle for justice that took place mainly during the 1950s and 1960s. Its purpose was for Black Americans to gain equal rights under the law in the United States.

The civil rights movement didn't start with a politician having a warm heart or leadership. It was led primarily by Martin Luther King Jr. and others, and then spread by ordinary citizens, not politicians.

## Unlikely Heroes

In August, 1994 civil rights leader Rosa Parks was robbed and beaten in her home in Detroit. At the age of eighty-one, she was robbed of fifty-three dollars by a man named Joseph Skipper. Skipper was a career criminal who knew Parks was the iconic figure of history books. Despite that knowledge, he punched Parks in the face. "Enter stage right," comes an unlikely hero. Mike Ilitch, the owner of Little Caesars Pizza, the Detroit Tigers Baseball Team, and the Detroit Red Wings Hockey Team stepped in to help. After reading about the assault and how a local federal judge secured an apartment for Parks in a safer area with security, Ilitch paid for Parks' apartment for more than a decade until her death in 2005 at the age of ninety-two. The story became public only after Ilitch's death in 2014.[20]

Based on Rosa Park's contribution to the civil rights movement and to the country, there are a list of people and organizations that should have stepped forward, from the National Association for the Advancement of Colored People (NAACP) to Al Sharpton or even the thirty-year congressman from Detroit, John Conyers. However, it was the first-generation American success story that was the hero of the hour. The point is, we are constantly told and almost forced to accept that identity politics is the new normal. Identity politics robs us of our American identity and we miss opportunities to accept and treat each other as fellow Americans. I urge you not to comply with their divisive agenda.

Unlikely heroes like Ilitch have occurred from the dawn of time.

After the Battle of the Milvian Bridge in 312 AD, Christianity gradually became the state religion. This not only brought religious toleration for Christians, but also a special status. Soon churches and cathedrals were springing up all over the Roman Empire. They became the center of communities and the sick often received treatment there.

The first hospitals were built in association with Christian basilicas. They were part of the churches' efforts to help the poor, which was a religious obligation. Local bishops were the driving forces behind these institutions.

---

20  https://www.usatoday.com/story/news/nation-now/2017/02/16/little-caesars-founder-mike-ilitch-rosa-parks-rent/97989230/

There is no agreement on who built the first hospital, but it is claimed that Leontius of Antioch built one between the years of 344 to 358. At around the same time, possibly with the support of the emperor, a deacon was placed in charge of the hospitals in Constantinople. This would suggest that hospitals run by Christians had been established even earlier than the mid-fourth century AD.[21]

When I look at adoptions and other humanitarian organizations, I usually see it was people of faith who started them. Because of their faith, they adopt children of other ethnicities, children who don't look like them. Because of their adherence to the teachings in the Bible, they care for widows and orphans. That is why Sheila and I adopted one of the five of our children. We often say we can't remember which one because we love them all the same.

## SOME PEOPLE GET MADD

Thirteen-year-old softball all-star Cari Lightner was killed May 3, 1980, when a three-time repeat offender was barreling down the road. Out of jail just two days from a fourth DUI arrest, he hit Cari from behind, throwing her out of her shoes 125 feet. He fled the scene but was later arrested and charged with her death.

Cari's mother, Candace Lightner, carried her daughter's photo with her as she worked tirelessly to change drunk driving laws in California. She wanted to try and make sense of a senseless act and turn her pain into purpose.[22]

---

21  https://classicalwisdom.com/culture/history/christianity-and-the-rise-of-the-hospital-in-the-ancient-world/
22  https://madd.org/our-history/

The DUI laws were not changed because politicians thought they should do something. They were changed because of a mom who lost her teenage daughter to a repeat offender and said enough is enough. She galvanized a group of women and established MADD, Mothers Against Drunk Driving, and that changed the DUI laws.

The Hunger Project, Charity Water, and Hope for Justice are other examples. Around the world, organizations are run by ordinary people who have taken leadership positions. They are solving the world's problems with no politics or federal government involvement. Volunteers donate, contribute, or lead nonprofit organizations that feed hungry, thirsty, and abused children globally more than any government entity around the world. And hardly anyone sees the good they do.

## THE POLARIZATION OF BLACK AMERICANS

W. E. B. DuBois was an American sociologist, historian, author, editor, and activist. He was considered the most important Black protest leader in the United States during the first half of the twentieth century. He shared in the creation of the NAACP in 1909 and was the first Black person to earn a PhD from Harvard. For more than a decade he devoted himself to sociological investigations of Blacks in America.

Although DuBois had originally believed that social science could provide the knowledge to solve the race problem, he gradually came to the conclusion that in a climate of virulent racism, expressed in such evils as lynching, peonage, disfranchisement, Jim Crow segregation laws, and race riots, social change could be accomplished *only through agitation and protest*. In this view, he clashed with the most influential Black leader of the period, Booker T. Washington. Washington preached a philosophy of accommodation, urging Blacks to accept discrimination for the time being and *elevate themselves through hard work and economic gain*. Washington's premise was that the large population of former slaves and their children were largely illiterate. They needed a foundation of education, a Christian moral compass, and an understanding of capitalism, agriculture, and the professional trades for self-sufficiency before taking political fights.

In 1903, in his famous book *The Souls of Black Folk*, DuBois charged that Washington's strategy, rather than freeing the Black man from oppression, would serve only to perpetuate it. This attack mistakenly crystallized the opposition to Booker T. Washington among many Black intellectuals, polarizing the leaders of the Black community into two wings, the conservative supporters of Washington and his radical critics.

DuBois, an open supporter of communism, also believed in what was called the Talented Tenth. He used the term to describe the likelihood of one in ten Black men becoming leaders of their race. He saw this group influencing the world through methods such as continuing their education, writing books, or becoming directly involved in social change. He strongly believed that Blacks needed a classical education to be able to reach their full potential, rather than the industrial education promoted by Washington and some White philanthropists.

In his *Talented Tenth* essay, DuBois wrote, "The Negro race, like all races, is going to be saved by its exceptional men. The problem of education, then, among Negroes must first deal with the Talented Tenth; it is the problem of developing the Best of this race that they may guide the Mass away from the contamination and death of the Worst."[23]

In other words, that small group of people should be a ruling elite, and common people should simply follow their directions.

Booker T. Washington was an educator and reformer, the first president and principal developer of Tuskegee Normal and Industrial Institute (now Tuskegee University), and the most influential spokesman for Black Americans between 1895 and 1915.

He was born in a slave hut, but after emancipation he moved with his family to Malden, West Virginia. Dire poverty ruled out regular schooling. At age nine he began working, first in a salt furnace and later in a coal mine. In 1872, determined to get an education, he enrolled at the Hampton Normal and Agricultural Institute (now Hampton University) in Virginia, working as a janitor to help pay expenses. He graduated in 1875 and returned to Malden, where for two years he taught children in a day school and adults at night. Following studies at Wayland Seminary, Washington, D.C. (1878–79), he joined the staff of Hampton.

In 1881, Washington was selected to head a newly established normal school for African Americans at Tuskegee, an institution with two small, converted buildings, no equipment, and very little money. Tuskegee Normal and Industrial Insti-

---

23   https://aaregistry.org/story/the-talented-tenth-a-definition/

tute became a monument to his life's work. At his death thirty-four years later, it had more than one hundred well-equipped buildings, some 1,500 students, a faculty of nearly 200 teaching thirty-eight trades and professions, and an endowment of approximately two million dollars.

Washington believed that the best interests of Black people in the post-Reconstruction era could be realized through education in the crafts, industrial skills, and the cultivation of the virtues of patience, enterprise, and thrift. He urged his fellow Blacks, most of whom were impoverished and illiterate farm laborers, to temporarily abandon their efforts to win full civil rights and political power and instead, to cultivate their industrial and farming skills so as to attain economic security.

Booker T. Washington's work in the field of education gave access to new hope for thousands of African Americans, many of them former slaves and children of slaves. By 1913, at the dawn of the administration of Woodrow Wilson, Washington had largely fallen out of favor. He remained at the Tuskegee Institute until congestive heart failure ended his life on November 14, 1915. He left behind a vastly improved Tuskegee Institute with over 1,500 students, a faculty of 200, and an endowment of nearly two million dollars to continue to carry on its work.[24]

Washington provided vocational education because that was what the market required at the time. The market didn't need a slew of Black scholars who could speak French and recite the periodic table. With no official title, Booker raised millions of

---

24   https://www.history.com/topics/black-history/booker-t-washington

dollars to help educate kids in the South. The founder of Sears & Roebuck donated money to build 5,000 elementary schools throughout the South.

After writing his autobiography, he was invited to Buckingham Palace to meet the Queen of England. He also served as an advisor to President Theodore Roosevelt. He was solutions oriented, solving problems instead of ranting about them. Sadly, he can be considered the first conservative to become a victim of cancel culture. His work, accomplishments, and beliefs are marginalized into the dark corner of American history. Progressive leftists, including Black leftists, demonize the man.

DuBois focused on forcing equal rights. He aimed to convince Blacks they were being used and abused by this racist country. He was responsible for the genesis of the conversation on racism we have today. He was an intellectual, and he was jealous of the influence Washington had on the Black community and beyond. DuBois was responsible for creating the first cancel culture victim for a conservative Black leader. He perpetuated the stigma that Washington was a sell-out and a tool of the White man.

The conversation is basically the same today. I see many people complaining and blaming and posting negative opinions online. Few people appear dedicated to coming up with solutions to the problems we're currently facing. Most kids growing up with no father in the home don't have the life skills needed to flourish in the world. Some of today's Black population is still trying to force equality, while others are working to establish ourselves as productive members of society. It's as if DuBois and Washington are still at odds with each other, still polarizing the population.

However, if Black America followed the directives of Booker T. Washington's teachings and business principles, Blacks would be in a much better position today and our country would be much better for it.

## TRANSCENDING POLITICS

If the Black population had followed Booker T. Washington's teaching, I believe we would be a completely different community and proud Americans today. But Washington's achievements and philosophy have been nearly wiped out of school textbooks and American history. Most Black people and very few White people know the name of Washington but have little to no idea of his significant achievements and ideals.

Today, it's not only the Black population that is being manipulated. There is a growing division between the elite political and secular class and the working middle class and lower income class.

## THE SOURCE OF LASTING CHANGE

It doesn't take 50 percent or a majority of the population to initiate positive change. It only takes 25-30 percent of the people. I recall my history teacher mentioning that during the American Revolution, one-third of the people wanted a free and independent country, one-third of the people wanted to remain as subjects to the King of England, and one-third of the population was too preoccupied to have an opinion. Two-thirds of the population benefitted because one-third took the risk and the exposure to drive toward a free country.

MADD didn't have half the moms in the country. They only had a few dedicated mothers. MLK didn't start out with thousands of influencers. Booker T. Washington had more opposition than support.

It takes a dedicated few fighting for what is right, to stand for a noble cause, something true and authentic, for the good of everyone. Often, those are God-centered beliefs and ideals. It's not political issues that help to sway things in our favor, but that's what we need now. That's what we are building with Take-Charge for the Black community and America overall. Every month, more people come, unsolicited, to help with our cause. They watch and see what we're doing, and they feel drawn to be part of it.

Americans tend to think electing a new president will change everything, but history has shown that most of the significant changes in society were made by unelected, everyday Americans. Likewise, Jesus was never elected to office, nor did He command an army or accumulate wealth. Yet our calendars are set from His birth and death and billions of people have followed His teaching for centuries.

I hold Booker T. Washington in high esteem, and I want to replicate what he was doing one hundred years ago. The kids who graduated from Tuskegee were getting jobs throughout the South before there was any diversity initiative or affirmative action because they had a skill the market needed. He focused his students on being virtuous, hardworking, and thrifty. He steered them toward business and entrepreneurship.

Take Charge exists to empower people to take charge of their own lives and the lives of their children without relying on the government or politicians for redemption and prosperity. We are determined to help people see they don't have to give up their identity to embrace their American citizenship and values. They should be proud of their history and what their ancestors overcame so that they can prosper today.

At TakeCharge, we are a beacon of truth, helping people to see through the murky water of politics, deception, and lies. Our volunteers are helping by communicating the changes in their own lives to their peers. We have Black women speaking to other Black women about how they have broken the chains of poverty. We have Black men speaking to other Black men, teenagers, and students about getting an education, getting married, and having children, in that order. We are developing the largest video library of Black Americans calling for a return to faith, family, and education, as well as denouncing progressive ideology. We are building a coalition of community champions, academic professionals, and business leaders to ignite a transformation within the Black community by embracing the core principles of America, not rejecting them.

When we're all swimming in the same tank, thinking, believing, and behaving the same way, it seems unnatural to swim in a new direction. But we don't have to stick with the popular paradigm. We can make changes in how we think and act without changing who we are. We can change our value structure and come home to who we're meant to be. As I said before, this is a prodigal project. We're the ones who left our faith, our traditional family structure, and our education, and we can be the people calling for a transformation back to the basics.

It is important to focus on the fundamentals to restore broken families. It's like being in a dark hallway in a building and all you can see is the exit sign. Not everyone sees it, but a few people are beginning to run toward it. That's what TakeCharge is. When enough people notice and join those running toward the exit sign, then more people will follow. With God on our side, we will begin to see the redemption of a culture in crisis, and see it in our lifetime.

Together, we can be the source of lasting change.

# TAKE CHARGE!

Throughout this book, I've shared my story and the stories of people who are helping to shift the conversation of victimhood to victory. You can see the root of the problems we face, and you're now aware of some possible solutions. Now it's your turn to get involved and take charge.

Start now. Please don't put this book down thinking it was a nice story or kind of inspirational. Don't walk away with your eyes open to the pervasive evil plaguing our culture. You have an opportunity now to initiate real-world results. If you are willing to act on the insights and awareness you now have, I promise your life will be richer for your efforts and generosity.

You might be thinking, "That sounds great, Kendall, but who am I to make a difference in such big problems? I'm nobody."

Well, join the club. I've always thought of myself as a nobody, too. I'm just a regular guy who cares about people. Thankfully, God always chooses nobodies to bring about change. The biblical story of Gideon also illustrates how God uses nobodies to create radical change. Gideon was named the fifth judge over Israel. We find him collecting wheat and hiding it from the enemy in Judges 6. As he was threshing wheat, an angel spoke to him and called him a mighty warrior. Gideon responded that he was a nobody. He came from a poor family and insisted he was not a hero. Some people say he spoke out of fear, but perhaps his response was one of humility. I imagine many people were hiding at home and possibly starving as the Midianites were besieging the land (Judges 6:1-6), yet Gideon was actively doing something for his people.

The angel also said Gideon would save Israel (Judges 6:14) because God was sending him to lead Israel into battle and lead the country to victory.

Gideon called on some men from the surrounding area to join him and build an army against the Midianites. He was sure God wanted him to lead that group of men, but God said he had recruited too many. God wanted Israel to know that it was not the might of 32,000 men that saved Israel, but God Himself. So, God told Gideon to send the men home who were afraid to go into battle. Twenty-two-thousand men turned around and walked away, and Gideon was left with 10,000 brave men (Judges 7:2-3).

A 10,000-man army is just what military strategists would agree was needed. However, God wanted it known that the battle was won by His will, not by Gideon and or the heroic deeds of the 10,000 men. He directed Gideon to go into battle with only 300 men to fight against the Midianites (Judges 7:4-8). According to Judges 8:10, there were at least 135,000 enemy troops against Gideon's 300 soldiers.

To make a long story short, Gideon and his army of 300 pursued their adversaries until they captured the enemy kings and princes. Their victory won the respect of the Hebrew nation. The fear of Gideon and his men then became great enough that Israel lived in peace and worshiped God for the next forty years until Gideon's death (Judges 8).

Gideon was a nobody who learned to trust God step by step. In the process, Gideon learned that God was in control. He obeyed God even when it seemed illogical to do so. His obedience was the foundation for his boldness because he chose to trust God even when he was uncertain that God would go before him and give him the victory. The point is, we all would be wise to trust in God, not in the conventional wisdom of popular culture and standards of accepted dogma.

## GET INVOLVED

I relate to Gideon because I was a nobody. I was a kid from Harlem, destined for drug use, violence, and prison like my siblings and some of my peers. Yet I broke out of the status quo and reshaped the narrative of my life with courage and determination.

As a teen, I had nobody to model my life after. When I became a Christian, I also became an avid reader. Initially, I read many of Pastor Tony Evans' books. When I became a father, I read Dr. James Dobson's books. I read countless books by Max Lucado. I also read Booker T. Washington's book, *Up From Slavery,* five times. These men, as well as women like Condoleezza Rice and Margaret Thatcher, influenced my character as a young man coming into adulthood.

By now, you can see that fatherless homes are the number one problem in the Black community. There has never been one national initiative to reverse the trend until now with our Prodigal Project at TakeCharge.

As of the writing of this book, we have fifty-one volunteers who have stepped forward to help transform the Black community to its historical roots of faith, family, and securing a better education for their children. We also have many people supporting our organization from the sidelines financially, as well as through prayer and moral support. Here's what some of them have to say about being involved in our cause:

"Thank you so much for answering your call to inspire all people to take charge of their lives! You and Sheila are beacons to light the way, powerful examples of belief in one's God-given talent and ability to forge a life of one's choosing, and in service to others. My wife and I believe in you, as demonstrated proof of the fruits of hard work, strong faith, and devotion to family, as well as an accomplished executive who can shepherd an idea into a reality. We are delighted to follow your leadership." —Scott L.

"I am excited about this program. You and your family are awesome. Thanks so much from an older White woman who respects and honors your work." —Kim B.

"This is so needed across the board . . . Do you have any chapters or affiliation in Ohio? I would love to volunteer my time and effort. I grew up without my father, but I am blessed and grateful to have broken that cycle with my son. I would love to share what I can. Thanks, and prayers for your organization!" —Michael R.

"This organization has an *excellent* mission and deserves much higher visibility in all communities, as it provides an alternative solution that includes *everybody*." —Dean D.

"Since returning to Minnesota in 2020, following a long absence, I have been discouraged with the actions of many in the state of my origin. You give me hope. May God watch over you." —Rand H.

"As a former special education teacher of "emotionally disturbed" children in a high crime area in Brooklyn, NY, I can attest firsthand to the urgency of the need for cultural changes mostly for Black inner-city kids and their mostly single-parent families. The problem is enormous, but rarely do I hear it addressed. Congrats to you for addressing the core of the problem, fatherlessness in the Black community and in other minority groups. And for mentioning faith-based education as well because that is also pitifully lacking in this country. I applaud your efforts to bring this to people's attention." —Cynthia B.

"This mission is far more important and far-reaching than any elective public office. You're doing God's work, and your mission is in my prayers." —Michael B.

We feel blessed and encouraged by the number of people coming alongside us in various ways. By now, maybe you are wondering how you can contribute to redeeming our culture in crisis. Here are some suggestions:

- Educate yourself on Black history that is rarely promoted
    - Read Booker T. Washington's book, *Up From Slavery*
    - Read how the Great Society, social welfare, and other government programs have decimated the Black family
- Support school choice for inner-city families to get them out of schools that leave high school graduates illiterate
- Get involved in a good Bible-teaching church
- If you're married, stay married and enroll in marriage enrichment workshops once a year
- Support us at TakeCharge (https://takechargemn.com/) and share links to our extensive video library with family, friends, and organizations that serve inner-city youth

Regardless of what you choose to do, make sure you get involved in some capacity. Get in action and watch how your life is enriched in the process. Not only will you flourish in your own life, but you'll have a front row seat to positive change in the world around you.

It's easy to stand off to the side and complain about the problems we're all facing. It's easy to be critical of the politicians, government programs, and heartless people who seem to be destroying humanity from the ground up. But getting involved will change your life, improve the lives of others, and help turn the tide for our country. In the process, you'll learn new skills, tackle proverbial giants, and grow in confidence. You'll be a bold champion for the oppressed.

The Bible says it this way: "If you do away with the yoke of oppression, with the pointing finger and malicious talk, and if you spend yourselves in behalf of the hungry and satisfy the needs of the oppressed, then your light will rise in the darkness, and your night will become like the noonday. The LORD will guide you always; he will satisfy your needs in a sun-scorched land and will strengthen your frame. You will be like a well-watered garden, like a spring whose waters never fail. Your people will rebuild the ancient ruins and will raise up the age-old foundations; you will be called Repairer of Broken Walls, Restorer of Streets with Dwellings" (Isa. 58:9b-12).

Amid uncertainty and chaos, we can be certain that fulfillment in life comes not by force but by being a contribution to society and loving the unlovable among us. I pray you'll make a commitment right now to take one meaningful action today. A culture in crisis awaits.

Finally, to quote the encouraging words of the character Maximus in the movie *Gladiator*, I leave you with these departing words: "Strength and honor."

# ABOUT THE AUTHOR

Kendall Qualls is a former Candidate for Governor of Minnesota and was recently reinstated as President of TakeCharge. TakeCharge strives to unite Americans regardless of background toward a shared history and common set of beliefs. Despite challenges and turmoil in his early life, Mr. Qualls served as an officer in the U.S. Army and earned three graduate degrees, including an MBA from the University of Michigan. He worked his way up the ranks at several Fortune 100 healthcare companies before he became Global Vice President of an $850 million business unit.

Mr. Qualls champions the principles of meritocracy and supports the notion that free enterprise, and the private sector are the fastest and most equitable way to lift people from poverty to prosperity. Mr. Qualls' articles have been published in the *New York Post*, *Washington Times*, *The Federalist*, Real Clear Politics, *The Christian Post*, and the *Minneapolis Star Tribune*. Mr. Qualls has been married to his wife, Sheila, for 37-years and they have five children together.

# A free ebook edition is available with the purchase of this book.

**To claim your free ebook edition:**

1. Visit MorganJamesBOGO.com
2. Sign your name CLEARLY in the space
3. Complete the form and submit a photo of the entire copyright page
4. You or your friend can download the ebook to your preferred device

A **FREE** ebook edition is available for you or a friend with the purchase of this print book.

CLEARLY SIGN YOUR NAME ABOVE

**Instructions to claim your free ebook edition:**
1. Visit MorganJamesBOGO.com
2. Sign your name CLEARLY in the space above
3. Complete the form and submit a photo of this entire page
4. You or your friend can download the ebook to your preferred device

## Print & Digital Together Forever.

Snap a photo

Free ebook

Read anywhere